D1649301

When Courage Is Not Enough

BRING YOUR "A" GAME

WILLIAM DOCK WALLS

OXYMORON PUBLISHING, CHICAGO

When Courage
Is Not Enough

BRING YOUR "A" GAME

William Dock Walls

Published by the Oxymoron Publishing Group
Oxymoron Group (USA)
47 West Polk Street, Suite 100-255, Chicago, Illinois 60605, U.S.A.

William Dock Walls
When Courage Is Not Enough

ISBN Number; 978-1-4276-3152-7

Printed in the United States of America on recycled paper

www. Whencourageisnotenough.com

www.Williamdockwalls.com

dockwalls2@aol.com

First Edition

Book design by American Shirt Company

Cover photo by: David Jenkins

ACKNOWLEDGEMENTS

Thanks be to God for the inspiration and the ability.

To every person who has ever dreamed of freedom.

To my wife Pamela.

To my children Anika, William, and Ashley; and my five granddaughters.

To my sisters, my brother, my family, friends and anyone who has ever supported anything I have ever done.

To my mother, Mary Walls-Jackson who, for years, walked to and from work to provide the staples our family needed.

To my father, William Walls, Jr., who hustled and took risks to furnish our family with prospects for greater opportunity.

God bless you one and all.

No matter what you are going through, Relax; God can suspend all of those things we call deadlines.

CONTENTS

INTRODUCTION

*T*rainers use psychological means to condition baby elephants for captivity. They simply drive a small stake in the ground, attach a chain to it and place the chain around that baby elephant's neck. Initially, that baby elephant will tug at the chain and try in vain to break free. That baby elephant will eventually come to the conclusion that it does not have the ability to tear free from that small stake in the ground, and give up on the freedom effort, never to try again. Even after that elephant is full-grown, and is able to uproot trees, it will not attempt to free itself by uprooting that small stake from the ground.

Similarly, our children are being conditioned to accept security screenings and view them as a fact of life. Many schools have metal detectors at the entrance. They were allegedly installed to keep our children safe from one another. But there are still knives in the lunchrooms, heavy tools in vocational classes, big books that could be used as blunt instruments, and every student carries at least one pen.

Just the other day, a child was shot outside the entrance to a school. The people met at city hall. Someone in their zeal suggested "We can place the metal detectors outside of the entrance to the school." The people enthusiastically said "yes." Someone more thoughtful suggested, "Let's really make it safe and place metal detectors around the entire perimeter of the school." In response the people roared an approval. Someone else reasoned, "One child might stand just outside the school's perimeter and shoot another. Therefore, we should put metal detectors at every local school bus stop." The people were on fire, enthused by these great suggestions that they believed would keep the children safe.

As the people, buzzing with excitement, started to leave, someone yelled, "Wait. What if a child decides to shoot another child while waiting for the bus to arrive?" Someone else asked "And what if the person seeking to harm a child is not another child, but an adult?" "Good point," they murmured as they settled back into their seats. "Eureka," someone exclaimed. "We'll place metal detectors outside of every residence and have everyone submit to a search before they can leave their home." Although reluctant, the people agreed to this suggestion. How could they not? After all they had agreed to all of the other ridiculous suggestions.

This silly but serious illustration highlights the lack of an endgame to America's current Security craze. We're on that proverbial, "slippery slope," and on track to become a nation on total lock-down. Americans have begun to accept maximum security as the norm, and have the nerve to look at citizens who resist the imposition of extraordinary security as strange.

There is no such thing as a coincidence. In the secular sense, things happen when preparation, opportunity and action collide. In the spiritual sense all things happen according to God's perfect will.

CHAPTER 1

MAN'S INGENUITY

Prehistoric Man was an autarky - *a wholly independent human being.* This hunter/fisherman would kill an animal with a stone, and eat its raw meat with his bloody hands. Man carried food home to his wife and children, each and every evening. The eating ritual was a bonding activity enjoyed by the entire family.

Any unfinished business would have to wait. The small amount of light emanating from the moon was not enough to permit Man to move safely about in the wilderness. So, within minutes of sunset the family unit was fast asleep in its cave.

One discovery led to another. Man produced stone tools about two and a half million years ago; learned to control fire a million years later; and invented the wheel in Mesopotamia around 3,500 B.C. Man's increased sophistication was self-perpetuating.

1

During the Stone Age, about 2,500 B.C., Man confessed to Mr. Jones his desire to work smarter. They grew to realize they shared common interests. Man and Mr. Jones formed a community just north of the Thames River. There was safety in numbers.

Pressured to keep up with the Joneses, Man and Woman moved into a bigger cave, up the hill. Woman wanted Man to manicure the lawn and chop down the excess bush. Man developed tools to make his chores easier.

The community grew and the people shared ideas. Two heads proved to be better than one. Working together, the people figured out how to do some things that had never been done before. They built shelter, waterholes and pits.

Many leaders emerged through the process of community development. A Leader is *"one with the proclivity to instantly recognize a need or a threat; Immediately ascertain and evaluate all facts and circumstances; develop, articulate and disseminate a timely, effective and efficient course of action; and empower, equip, inspire and motivate others to act unselfishly in pursuit of the greater good."*

About 800 B.C., Man, Mr. Jones and the people of the community used wooden bowls and spoons. Circa 750 B.C. Woman wanted a new dress because Mrs. Jones wore a different one the day before. To accommodate Woman's desire, Man developed textile production. Man also surprised Woman with a finely designed Bronze trinket.

Man slowly developed into a sophisticated being, not by necessity, but by virtue of ingenuity. Man refused to be outdone by Mr. Jones. Every time Mr. Jones got a whistle Man had to have a whistle and a bell.

From fishing to hunting and fighting, everything became a leadership competition. Life was the season. At the end of his season, when Man closed his eyes for good, the people counted the number of leadership beads he had earned. The Man that earned more leadership beads than all who had preceded him was assured a place in the Golden Book.

You will not be listed in the Golden Book because of your wealth. Money only matters when everyone else has some, and you ain't got none.

CHAPTER 2

GOLDEN BOOK

*T*here is a Golden Book that heralds those who cared enough to become socially significant. It memorializes the first responders who heard the cries of others at risk and rushed in to confront the danger. That Golden Book is imprinted in the hearts and minds of men and women whose lives have been touched by those selfless heroes who dared to make a difference.

Once your name is written in the Golden Book you can rest assured; your living shall not have been in vain. The names written therein resound in hallowed quarters where hope lives and legacies are immortalized. People can take your worldly possessions, but no one can erase your name once it's written in the Golden Book.

Whether willing to admit it or not, everyone aspires to be recognized. Everyone wants to leave footprints in the sand. Children etch their names in freshly poured concrete so that they might be remembered. Taggers paint their logos on train boxcars, which are transported around the world, in an attempt to immortalize themselves.

People will kill for money; but people will die for recognition. A common robber will murder anyone who stands between he and the loot. Yet, the bank guard will give up his life to protect the unsuspecting. The greed, which threatens our civility, is counterbalanced by the courage, which has made our society great.

No matter how much money you make during the course of your lifetime, you can't take it with you. The Brink's truck will not join your funeral procession and follow the Hearst to the cemetery. Your heirs will toast to your financial success even as they erase your name from the bank account. Soon it will be as if you never even existed.

However, if you fought to make the world a better place, someone will remember you. When future generations gather to recognize those who've made outstanding contributions to society, someone will mention your name. Your money only matters as long as you're here; but you will forever matter once your name is in the Golden Book.

People mistakenly believe that Politics, the Macropolitic, and Government are all one and the same. Although inextricably intertwined and interdependent in many ways, they are three distinct and different animals.

CHAPTER 3

BEYOND POLITICS

While earning my Bachelor of Science degree in Political Science from Tuskegee Institute, located in Macon County, Alabama, I was taught by Professor Gwen Williams that, *"Politics is who gets what; when where and how."* That succinct definition of politics is universally accepted and taught in most intuitions of higher learning.

However, after years of practical involvement as an activist, I came to realize that, although popular, that scant definition of politics is too passive. It fails to acknowledge that politics is an intentional force. No action is political unless someone does something deliberate.

In our uniquely well-ordered, well-structured society, things don't just happen by chance. Things don't evolve or develop in a vacuum;

things happen by design. Things happen when people with a plan act purposefully.

In light of this, I ventured to absolutely define the term Politics. My goal was to completely demarcate the essence of this effervescent mean, and distinguish it from similar mediums of interaction. Eventually, I arrived at the optimal definition.

Politics is *"the personification of a deliberate effort to develop a relationship, create a perception, influence a decision, or otherwise determine who has to pay, who gets to play, and who has the final say; whether in the boardroom, courtroom or on the streets."*

The requisite "deliberate effort" is evidenced by direct action, the dissemination of information, an attempt at organization, or any other identifiable means of purposeful manipulation.

-1-

THE MACROPOLITIC

As I mentioned, for something to be political a person must engage in some action. However, beyond the concept of simple politics there is a stimulus that lives and breeds in every populated environment. It affects all things and all circumstances. This naturally occurring force transcends conscious activity.

When the doctor taps your knee with a rubber hammer, you automatically kick, in response to a normal biological reflex. This political force is the social equivalent of that biological reflex. It exists in a vacuum and precedes any and all other actions.

This force is an all-encompassing dynamic conflagration fueled by instinct. Its essence invades our homes, churches workplaces, neighborhoods, and our streets. This force inspires decisions concerning the clothes we wear and the food we eat.

Despite the breadth and depth of the American political lexicon, prior to now, no one has identified a term for this force. Thus, I've chosen to call it the "Macropolitic." The Macropolitic is defined as *"the base inspiration for a political response."*

Now that I have identified and defined the Macropolitic, I will describe it and put it into perspective, to help you fully appreciate its magnitude.

The Macropolitic should not be confused with survival instincts like fight or flight or an animal's instinct to eat. Although innate, those reactions are neurological in nature. The chemical

Adrenaline triggers the fight or flight response. The organs in mammal and animal bodies send a signal to the brain, which results in the urge to eat. That being then relies upon the sense of smell to lead it to food.

An amoeba is a microscopic one-celled organism whose cytoplasm and organelles are enclosed within a single cell membrane. An amoeba instinctively moves, feeds on particles and reproduces. The unintelligent amoeba does not think, but simply reacts to stimuli in its environment. For example, an amoeba automatically adjusts its own composition to compensate for the amount of saline in the water.

The Macropolitic should not be confused with the Body Politic, which refers to any group, governed by any means. The Macropolitic is not government. You don't engage the Macropolitic it engages you.

Like Mother Nature, the Macropolitic is an uncontrollable, incontrovertible force. The Macropolitic is a ubiquitous agency active wherever there are at least two live beings in contact or communication.

For example, if an unarmed man and a bear were inhabitants on an otherwise forsaken island, the Macropolitic would influence their behavior. Once aware of each other's existence, the man would instinctively endeavor to avoid the bear and, thus, stay alive. Whereas, consistent with its beastly predatory nature, the bear would seek to confront the man.

-2-

POWER POLITICS

Exceptional leaders have adequate, if not impeccable, organizational skills and are adroit at thinking on their feet. Both of these attributes are powerful. A leader who lacks either of these qualities is at best average. Well-organized, persistent individuals are more likely to have what it takes to prevail. These are the ones who engage in Power Politics – *the continuation of purposeful activities beyond the customary limits of political achievement.*

Throughout history, the Macropolitic has propelled the curious nature exhibited by mammals, animals and entire countries. These intrinsic curiosities have invariably led to exploration, which often resulted in domination and colonization. Some have demonstrated an uncanny ability to become lord and master of all they encounter.

In both the animal and mammal sense, if you want to find out who's got it and who ain't, toss a chew toy into a kennel full of puppies or a rattler into a nursery full of infants and watch the action. Some will ignore that foreign object. But, the alert courageous ones will instantly cease their whimpering and whining and compete for control of it. They will chew on it, bang on it and manipulate it to determine what it is, what it does, and what it is capable of. The ones who continue to explore that object long after the others have lost interest are more prone to Power Politics.

-3-

GOVERNMENT

Government is *"a hierarchy of respected relationships interacting to create enforceable laws."* Government's mandate is to provide for the common defense; ensure civility; and to take care of those who are weak, afflicted, infirmed or disoriented.

Pursuant to that limited mandate, Government delivers a myriad of authorized services paid for by revenue derived from taxation, and the assessment and collection of fines and fees. Taxpayers intend for their collective funds to be used for the greater public good. They do not intend for that revenue to be used against them, or against their interest.

There are many types of government in effect around the globe. Chief among them are the Autocracy, Democracy, Dictatorships, Monarchy, and Republic. Each of these has variations, known by different names.

11

Democracy is premised upon the concept of majority rule. In a Democracy every eligible person may register and vote for the candidate or idea of their choice and the ones with the most votes win. While Democracy may seem fair, conceptually, it cannot guarantee equality.

The government officials who administer a Democracy have to abide by the decisions of the majority. They have no power or legal authority to protect the rights of voters who share the minority view, from the whims of the majority.

-4-

CONSTITUTIONAL REPUBLIC

Although America is often referred to as a Democracy, the word "Democracy" is not mentioned in the Constitution one single time. In fact, America is a Constitutional Republic, which provides for the administration of government in adherence to the Rule of Law as expressed in ratified constitutional doctrines. Under this model of government, the majority of voters cannot take away the inalienable rights of the minority.

The first three words of the Preamble to the U.S. Constitution are, "We the People." This expression of "popular sovereignty" affirms that the people, alone, are the source of government authority. The Legislature, Judiciary and Chief Executive are nothing more than three branches of government that provide a balance of power. The elected or appointed officials who sit in those seats serve at the behest of the people, and are bound by the Rule of Law.

The American Republic is a Representative form of government. As such, the individual State legislatures choose the method of selecting representatives that best suits them. That includes the selection of the members of the Electoral College, which alone elects the President.

The lack of citizen authority to elect a U.S. President was affirmed by the Supreme Court of the United States in George W. Bush *v.* Albert Gore, Jr. on December 12, 2000. That Court held:

> "The individual citizen has no federal constitutional right to vote for electors for the President of the United States unless and until the state legislature chooses a statewide election as the means to implement its power to appoint members of the Electoral College. U.S. Const., Art. II, §1. This is the source for the statement in *McPherson* v. *Blacker*, 146 U.S. 1, 35 (1892), that the State legislature's power to select the manner for appointing electors is plenary; it may, if it so chooses, select the electors itself, which indeed was the manner used by State legislatures in several States for many years after the Framing of our Constitution. *Id.*, at 28—33. History has now favored the voter, and in each of the several states the citizens themselves vote for

13

Presidential electors. When the state legislature vests the right to vote for President in its people, the right to vote as the legislature has prescribed is fundamental; and one source of its fundamental nature lies in the equal weight accorded to each vote and the equal dignity owed to each voter. The State, of course, after granting the franchise in the special context of Article II, can take back the power to appoint electors. See *id.,* at 35 ("[T]here is no doubt of the right of the legislature to resume the power at any time, for it can neither be taken away nor abdicated") (quoting S. Rep. No. 395, 43d Cong., 1st Sess.)."

Although America's government is not a true Democracy, many refer to it as such, because it employs democratic processes. The most notable of which is the electoral process. But like beauty, Democracy is in the eyes of the beholder.

Throughout the years, Americans have proposed several measures concerning the right to vote, which is commonly associated with the democratic electoral process. Thomas Jefferson would have a Democracy where only White men with property were allowed to vote. Andrew Jackson advocated for a Democracy that allowed all White men to vote. Dr. Martin Luther King promoted a Democracy that assured all men and women the right and ability to vote.

Painter Andy Warhol promised everyone fifteen minutes of fame. When you get yours, will you be a flash in the pan of financial success or linger in the limelight of social significance?

CHAPTER 4

GLORIOUS ARE THE BRAVE

Some people are born with a propensity for guerilla warfare. They constantly question authority, and tear down charming facades to reveal ugly inequities. Those crusaders have never encountered a righteous cause they didn't deem worthy of their time. They will not rest, slumber nor sleep until everybody is able to breathe free.

Some people will settle for nothing less than a world that embraces every person and a society that encourages everyone to achieve. Those idealists covet a just civilization where people are limited only by their ability. These humanitarians won't quit until human decency is the norm, and not an occasional deviation from it.

These Freedom Fighters don't just talk the talk; they walk the walk. They're the ones who instinctively spring from their cubbyholes and dart into harms way. Thank God for the courageous Freedom Fighters for they shall lead us into the Promised Land.

I respect warriors who eagerly throw caution to the wind, akin to the fictional Don Quixote who eagerly attacked a field of gigantic windmills. I applaud a warrior's willingness to risk being ridiculed for behaving atypically. After all, a leader who battles the status quo to ensure truth, justice, and fair play, knows there is a price to pay.

Sacrifice and commitment are laudable, but there are times when those fine qualities alone just won't do. There are times when sheer strength or persistent will is insufficient to get the job done. No matter how adept the warrior or how brave the combatant; there are times when courage is not enough.

Some people are leaders; some people are supporters; and some people are bobbleheads, just happy to be on the bus; with no concern for destination, route, or departure time.

CHAPTER 5

OF MEN AND MICE

Generally speaking, leadership is that group of people with the vision and skill necessary to successfully move a project, from conception to completion.

To be relevant, a leader must demonstrate an abiding appreciation for history and constantly study the political, technical, financial and geographical landscapes. Adept leaders constantly scan the horizon looking for abnormal occurrences.

Once a leader encounters an anomaly, they monitor its progress and assess its probable impact. By and large, leaders who do their homework are confident and decisive as well as prepared to strike at the most propitious instance.

Conversely, leaders who habitually wait until the last minute to prepare are more likely to err in judgment. Proverbially speaking, leaders who fly by the seat of their pants are cynical and less certain of the consequences of their actions. Therefore, they are more likely to succumb to pessimistic paralysis – *"a debilitating condition that results from inadequate preparation; evidenced by the inability to act timely and decisively."* He who hesitates may be lost; but he who becomes pessimistically paralyzed loses.

-1-

UNSELFISH SERVICE

Political Leaders are the advocates who are socially conscience, politically aware, and actively prosecuting a personal desire for social and political change.

Whereas it is acceptable for business leaders to be selfish and driven by greed, people expect political leaders to be unselfish - *altruistic rather than concerned about self-aggrandizement.* Business leaders seek to be noteworthy because of personal financial success. Unselfish political leaders aspire to achieve a social success, which for purposes of any discussion, may be defined as *"a lasting victory with broad civic implications."*

Dr. Martin Luther King, Jr. and Mahatma Gandhi, two of history's most magnanimous political leaders, are absolute shinning examples of altruism. These social giants, whose campaigns were waged decades and worlds apart, sought only to enrich society. They were living manifestations of the concept of social significance over financial success.

The reach of government is limited, thus there are some itches that government can't scratch. The work of Political leaders begins where government's reach ends.

-2-

REALISM OF PURSUITS

Conscientious leaders know their limitations. Rather than allow emotion to determine which causes they will address, they allow their real capacity and capabilities to dictate the breadth, depth and entire spectrum of their involvement. These leaders mindfully limit themselves to engagement in battles to which they can commit adequate time and resources.

A modest weekend warrior may dream big, but only have the capacity to address local issues; whereas, an equally modest full-time freedom fighter may be capable of mounting a viable worldwide campaign. The key is to bite off only as much as you can chew.

-3-

SUPPORTERS

Supporters are *"those ever-enthusiastic allies who share a common moral compass and goal."* These fanatical activists are indispensable in a movement or campaign. They fund the effort and rally for the cause. The average supporter not only has the capacity to lead but the modesty to acquiesce to leadership. Supporters who would be leaders understand that no one can lead all of the causes all of the time.

Thanks to technology and advanced forms of communication, today's supporters are better informed than ever before. They know the issues and all angles to the various arguments. They populate the tribunals that set the standards and outline the message. Thus, supporters not leaders are the driving force behind any modern movement.

Because of supporter sophistication, modern leaders simply determine the direction in which people are heading and get out in front to regulate the pace of the movement. In that sense a leader is like the director of an orchestra. Similar to trained musicians reading the sheet music, supporters play the notes. The leader stands before them to mark time, control the tempo and make certain everyone chimes in on schedule.

The supporters establish the end game. They determine the elements of an acceptable resolution, relative to a particular issue. When the vast majority of supporters are satisfied that the objective has been achieved, or are no longer willing to pursue the action, for all practical purposes, it's over. Because a leader without supporters is just another person with an opinion.

-4-

LEADERSHIP DEVELOPMENT

Many Supporters are leaders in training. One maxim suggests that to be a good leader, one must be a good supporter. Some have suggested that good leaders are nothing more than well-informed supporters who know the best route and best time to depart.

Realistic leaders realize they will not be around forever. They also realize struggles against deep-seated forces may be long and protracted. Odds are most issues may not be resolved during a single lifetime. Therefore committed leaders fight the battle and groom the next generation of leadership, simultaneously.

A common method of leadership development is the Mentor-Protégé Relationship. A mentor is an established craftsman who is willing to share their substantial experience with a beginner. The Protégé is a beginner in a particular field who

21

receives the advice and support of one who is established in that field of endeavor.

A good mentor will allow their protégé to assume a limited leadership role and monitor them closely. They will subjectively evaluate their performance, assess their effectiveness, and provide objective feedback. A mentor will gradually increase the protégé's responsibility in an effort to build their confidence.

-5-

BOBBLEHEADS

Although Americans donate large amounts of money to charitable causes, ours has still been labeled a "Bystander society." We wear that dubious distinction because there are far too many bobbleheads – *"selfish individuals who exhibit no desire to make a difference in society."*

Bobbleheads are apathetic bystanders with little or no sense of obligation to leave the world a better place. They are not committed to any activist cause, hardly participate in the electoral process and, on the extreme end, don't even believe it is their civic duty to vote.

Too often we hear reports of bobbleheads ignoring the pleas of victims being physically assaulted or robbed in broad daylight. Some are entertained by such tragic events. Those indifferent bobbleheads are content to sit idly by and watch others struggle to survive adverse or perilous situations. Sadly, most bobbleheads exhibit no regard for the fate of crime victims and refuse to cooperate with the police investigating those crimes.

While I can appreciate a bobblehead's desire to avoid risky interventions that could put them in harms way, I cannot understand their refusal to at least summons help. How difficult is it to dial 9-1-1? Although it is perfectly legal for people to stand by and do absolutely nothing, even a bobblehead has a moral obligation to provide the police with information that might help solve a crime. These bystanders could do it anonymously and, thereby, not compromise their own safety.

Unless a bobblehead has a "dog in the hunt" they are not likely to help another who is threatened or in imminent danger. However, when something or someone threatens their peaceful enjoyment of life, or their pursuit of happiness, they want everyone in the world to drop what they are doing and come to their rescue. Never mind the terrorist or foreign detractors, the ironically selfish behavior of bobbleheads is eroding the quality of life Americans relish.

The notoriously apolitical stance of bobbleheads is unacceptable. All Americans, including the bobbleheads, owe a tremendous debt of gratitude to the political leaders and supporters who fight to preserve the freedoms we enjoy. No matter which side of the issue an activist is on, whether we agree with them or not, we should celebrate their participation. That unadulterated respect for others shall keep America free.

Chances are, no advocate is absolutely right or totally wrong. For example, all reasonable people abhor discrimination. Activists on one side of the issue insist the remedy lies in affirmative action. Whereas, activists on the other side argue that affirmative action inherently results in reverse discrimination. As is the case with most issues, the truth lies somewhere in the middle.

However, as ugly as conflict is, it is a fact of life. Parties on opposite sides of an issue may never agree, and the discussion may grow loud and contemptuous. However, as long as the public discourse continues, society wins. When no one cares to debate the issues, apathy has overcome interest. When apathy reigns we all lose.

-6-

NO DEPOSIT NO RETURN

Like everyone else, bobbleheads pay taxes, which are required to fund government. In our society equal protection is the law of the land. So, theoretically, bobbleheads should receive the same services and protections afforded the most active citizens.

24

However, in reality, the squeaky wheel gets the grease. Elected officials monitor election results, sometimes on a precinct-by-precinct basis. They extrapolate from those numbers to determine where to concentrate their efforts and services.

A politician's allocation of resources and responsiveness to constituency concerns closely parallels constituent voting patterns. Undoubtedly, they are most responsive to their supporters, followed by those who vote, and least responsive to the bobbleheads who are the political equation group least likely to impact subsequent elections.

Like ostrich, bobbleheads bury their heads in the sand hoping to be overlooked by predators. That senseless strategy does not work in the African wild, and it certainly does not work in our dog-eat-dog society. No matter how inoffensive bobbleheads attempt to appear, the aggressors among us do not ignore them.

The rights of bobbleheads are violated and they are victimized as much as anyone else. The difference is they don't cultivate lasting alliances. Thus, bobbleheads usually stand alone when forced to resolve issues that adversely affect them.

There is no justification for a bobblehead's aversion to participation in the activities that safeguard America's freedoms.

Organization builds Confidence. Confidence yields Growth. Growth makes the possibilities real.

CHAPTER 6

EDGE OF ORGANIZATION

Organization is the keystone that results from planning. Without organization the best and the brightest are no more effective than a band of fools, prone to attack willy-nilly. The most reliable hope for measured success rests in a thoughtful strategy. The best hope for complete victory rests in a solution based, results oriented campaign.

The political landscape is a laboratory. Political Scientists conduct experiments to find the keys to victory. There is no substitute for the practical hands-on experience one gains only through participation in the political process.

Every election is an organizing opportunity. A committed organizer does not have the luxury of cherry picking elections. Whether as the candidate, or a supporter of one, the more you participate the more you grow. Never let the fear of losing, or your foolish pride, stand in the way of your growth opportunities.

People associate with and do business with people they know, like and trust. Establishing meaningful and substantive relationships is a time consuming process, without shortcuts. For those determined to make a difference in our society, every day is game day. There is no such thing as a day off. You can rest after you've taken your last breath.

-1-

CAMPAIGN DEVELOPMENT

Every major historical campaign has been developed in five fundamental stages. Those stages are the same whether the campaign was waged in Europe or America; whether waged by Aristocracy or Grassroots.

There are many ad hoc methods of campaign development that are not as extensive or demanding as the one I outline herein. No matter which method you utilize, the results will vary according to your aptitude. Although there is no absolute method, this tried and true process of campaign development has stood the test of time.

The five stages of campaign development are: Management, Message, Money, Media and Manpower. Each of these various stages are indispensable. Each stage should be cultivated according to this exact sequence.

Although, all of the stages will eventually operate simultaneously, a campaign should unfold stage by stage. The stage at hand should be allowed to surge until it has built up unstoppable momentum. Once that stage matures, the next stage of the campaign may be undertaken.

1. Management–the structured organization, and the leaders who develop the campaign's objectives, philosophy, methodology and message. Leaders train and direct supporters and furnish them with the tools necessary to accomplish each task.

2. Message–the definitive theme crafted by Management to express the purpose of the campaign, its agenda and its goals. Management should tweak this message until it is succinct and universal. All subsequent campaign statements and responses should be indivisible from this primary message.

3. Money–the capital to fund the publicity, provisions, resources and organizational infrastructure necessary to advance the cause and promote the definitive message.

4. Media–the paid and free mass communication mediums used to publicize the message, increase awareness, educate the public and aid in the recruitment of manpower.

5. Manpower–Supporters who are willing to work to accomplish the campaign objective.

-2-

MEETING MAGIC

In the past, effective leaders were forward thinking, keen eyed communicators with the oratorical ability to stir people's emotions and inspire them to act. Churches, bars, private homes and workplaces were the settings where most people commonly gathered to receive information and rally around causes. Those exciting boiler room environments - where emotions leapt from one person to another - were easy breeding grounds for political activism.

With the exception of churches, the traditional boiler room environments may be gone and lost forever. Much to the chagrin of traditionalists, more people work from home, socialize at home, eat at home, or frequent fast food drive-thru restaurants. Most people get their information via technology - phone, email or text message instead of actually gathering together.

Although Emailing, Blogging, Chatting and Posting are arguably interactive, these are comparatively impersonal means of communication. Modern leaders whether elected representatives or under-resourced warriors are challenged to stimulate people and drive them to action usually via text on a monitor.

In the short run, the most celebrated leaders of this decade may not be the sensational demagogues, but may very well be those that most quickly and ably text message. Fortunately, there is good news for those traditionalists who rue the steady advance of technology.

Video messaging will soon replace text messaging. Thus, modern leaders will virtually appear on the recipient's monitor and stylishly deliver a message in their own image and voice. Consequently, the most successful leaders of this millennium may still be those who are most rousing, attractive and compelling.

Movements are born of the synergy created when people of like minds gather together and meet. The magic is in the meeting. Every meeting is a mini campaign and should be conducted according to the five-stage process.

The Management is provided by the host of the meeting; The Message is delivered by the main speaker; The Money is amassed by the supporters in the form of sales, pledges or regular dues; The Media is embodied in the dissemination of literature; and The Manpower is derived from the volunteers and staff assigned responsibilities for completion prior to the next meeting.

Adherence to this formula assures infinite organization.

-3-

COALITIONS

There is nothing more disconcerting than the struggle of the disconnected. One-man-band demonstrations usually prove to be exercises in futility. Activists increase their chances for success when they pool their resources and aggressively form coalitions with others of like mind.

A Coalition is *"a merger of multiple parties with common philosophies and objectives."* These relationships are typically predicated upon a shared core mission. Whether they share the same primary objective or have different motives, parties coalesce because they regard the accomplishment of a particular mission as a means of advancing their own cause; or see it as key to achieving their ultimate goal.

Today's leaders, like their causes, do not exist in a vacuum. The likelihood of success in any venture is enhanced by addition, not subtraction. The concept of coalition enables joint leaders to accelerate the pace of the action and cover all bases as co-dependants.

To be relevant, leaders must involve themselves in a wide range of dissimilar causes. They must be good and capable supporters, willing to assist other leaders in their primary pursuits. The most

31

essential quality of a leader is the humility to play second fiddle.

Members of common labor pools form unions and other alliances. The individual workers who comprise those various groups are often driven by shared emotions. Alone they are weak insignificant and powerless to affect change, but united they have bargaining power.

Alliances made up of people who coalesce to protect their own individual interests are more effective and more resourceful than limited pay-to-play contractual relationships, or those purchased using the political largess.

Coalition partners may be likened to two airline passengers, without parachutes, whose combined fare's fuel the non-stop flight; their destination is one and the same. Each will contribute that which is necessary to ensure there is enough fuel to complete the trip.

Political Parties and their platforms reflect the interests and agenda of their active members. Passive people need not expect anything.

CHAPTER 7

ORGANIZED POLITICS

Organized politics is "the manifestation of an agreement between two or more entities, to operate within a well-defined structural framework, and execute a plan that is designed to achieve a certain political goal or result."

The most notable American political organizations are mammoth, well-staffed institutions, which hire professional consultants and have ongoing relationships with major advertising agencies. The largest political organizations have yearly budgets in the hundreds of millions of dollars and spend on par with some local governmental bodies. This includes our traditional political parties, campaign committees, lobbyist, Political Action Committees and other Special Interest groups.

Every instance of the Political Apparatus is private, exclusive and designed to benefit select individuals and certain groups of people. Political organizations have no public mandate or obligation. Unlike not-for-profit organizations, political organizations do not receive government grants or public funding. Political organizations are funded by contributions that are not tax-deductible. Private donors expect to increase their influence, and intend for their contributions to be used for partisan political purposes.

-1-

MODERN POLITICAL PARTIES

Although, there are many political parties in America, modern national elections are dominated by the Republican and Democratic Parties. Anti-slavery activists formed the Republican Party in 1854 in an effort to oppose the pro-slavery policies of the Democratic Party. Initially African Americans were loyal to the Republicans but, from 1932 to 1964, gradually transitioned their allegiance to the Democrats.

The Whig Party once deemed to be a major political party, elected Presidents William H. Harrison in 1840 and Zachary Taylor in 1848. However, no candidate put forth by any Independent Party has ever won the U.S. Presidency. With the exception of Presidential candidate billionaire Ross Perot, who ran in 1992 and 1996, no third Party candidate for national office has ever been seen as a serious candidate with the potential for victory. Thus, our political system is typically considered to be a two party system.

Arguably, it is difficult for the Green Party or any Independents to achieve a breakthrough because State and Federal election laws and accepted rules of engagement are most favorable to the two major parties. Additionally, mainstream media will not provide equal time to Independent or Green Party candidates.

Although neither Independents nor Third Party candidates have demonstrated the ability to win nationwide races, Independent Party candidates have won statewide races. For example, as a candidate of the Reform Party of Minnesota, Jesse "The Body" Ventura was elected that state's governor in 1988.

-2-

RED STATES, BLUE STATES

In recent years, American states have been politically described and categorized as either red or blue states, according to the philosophical tendencies of their voting aged population. States dominated by voters partial to the Republican Party are considered to be Red states. Whereas states dominated by voters aligned with the Democratic Party are identified as Blue states.

The Red state - Blue state categorization is a direct result of the Media's affinity for color-coded graphics and displays. Although this latest connotation may be expedient for visual aid purposes, the net effect is that it further divides the people of this nation.

This overall state classification casts aspersions on people whether they participate in organized politics or not. As soon as one identifies their state of residence, they are subject to stereotype based upon whether that state happens to be considered Red or Blue.

Admittedly, the Red state-Blue state tag is catchy. But like the phrase Hatfields vs. the McCoys that tag is utterly divisive. America just recently outgrew the stereotyping of people based upon whether they lived north or south of the Mason-Dixon Line. Absent those new colorful connotations, such political tinged assumption can only be made once you know a person's political party affiliation.

Meanwhile, Party loyalist are working overtime to convert Blue states into Red states, and vice-versa. Republicans seek to convince would-be Democrats that only the Republican Party embraces the values that Americans honor and cherish. Democrats seek to convince erstwhile Republicans that it's time for change in America.

"And the LORD God formed man of the dust of the ground, and breathed into his nostrils the breath of life; and man became a living soul."

Genesis 2:7

CHAPTER 8

AFRICAN SPRAWL

*I*rrespective of race, color, hair texture, facial features or language, people are all the same. All mankind originated in Africa. This is confirmed by modern genetic DNA evidence, physical and biological anthropology, and Paleoanthropology.

One of the first migrations of humans out of Africa occurred about one hundred and thirty thousand years ago when African hunters migrated north into the Levant region of the Middle East. This significant event was made possible by mutually occurring wet periods in the southern and northern regions of the hyper-arid Saharan-Arabian desert. Perhaps even more significant than that northern migration, was the southern migration of Africans into Asia.

According to Professor Alan Cooper, one of the preeminent leaders in the field of fragmentary

DNA research and Professor of Ancient Biomolecules at the University of Oxford,

"Research by Oxford University and collaborators has shed new light on the last 100,000 years of human migration from Africa into Asia. The new genetic study confirms that some of the earliest migrants traveled into Asia by a southern route, possibly along the coasts of what are now Pakistan and India." In the final analysis, Cooper said "The findings mark a significant step forward in our understanding of the nature and timing of human settlement of the world outside Africa, and may even give us a glimpse of what these ancient explorers looked like genetically."

About fifteen thousand years ago, Native Americans descended from Asian nomads. Those warrior-herders followed bison into North America, across the Bering Strait land bridge. That wide landmass was easily traversable when the sea level dropped 300 feet during, the Wisconsin Glacial episode. By the end of that ice age that bridge disappeared beneath the surface of the Bering Sea.

Those Paleo-Americans populated North America. Depending upon where they settled, they were known as Alaskan Natives, Native Americans, or Mixteco. As one, they flourished.

One person's junk is another person's treasure. Old junk can be traded for things that bring pleasure no one can measure.

CHAPTER 9

ENGLAND, BUILT TO LAST

*E*arly man believed the Earth was a land disc floating in water. One day an astronomer tossed out the suggestion that the world was not flat but instead was round. Eager adventurers picked up the mantle and set sail for far off places. The mundane waited for them to return and settled for listening to their stories of exotic places and strange people.

During the fifteenth century, European mariners sailed beyond their horizons in search of opportunity. The Portuguese, the most ambitious of all seafarers, became the leaders in world exploration. They demonstrated the courage to pursue their interest and follow their dreams. However, in the end courage was not enough to earn them status as the preeminent world conqueror.

The Portuguese were the consummate traders. They were interested in acquiring any tasty morsel, useful tool, or feel good artistic impression that might have trade value. In 1517, they forged into China and established an exclusive trade relationship with the Chinese. This enabled them to pedal silk fabric, rice and tea throughout Europe. Although treated badly by China's rulers, the Portuguese exhibited the fortitude necessary to maintain that beneficial relationship.

In 1620 although lacking the vision and raw courage of the Portuguese, the Dutch had the gumption to establish a colony in China. They conquered Taiwan and established a trading outpost there. They demonstrated their leadership potential by challenging China and seeking to control a portion of that intimidating country.

Until 1667, England was convinced that trade with China was of no real value. England began to import tea only after it became a popular drink in local coffeehouses. Parliament banned the importation of silk, as that item was perceived to be a threat to the England's textile industry.

England, a country retarded by it relationship with Spain, failed to see the value in trade beyond Europe. Hoisted by her own petard, England was a consumer not a trade connoisseur. However, despite England's shortcomings, when she finally developed an interest in colonization through world exploration, she exhibited an unmatched capacity. Before long, the sun was always shining on some colony of the British Empire.

-1-

FIVE STAGES OF ENGLAND'S CAMPAIGN FOR WORLD EXPLORATION

1. Management – by the beginning of the sixteenth century England had developed the most advanced government of any nation.

2. Message – England's message was embodied in the Magna Carta, which outlined the principles for which she stood. England had divorced herself from Spain and would seek her own identity in the New World.

3. Money – England enhanced her treasury by profitably transforming herself from an exporter of raw wool to an exporter of woolen cloth. Under Henry VII, England further enriched her coffers through more aggressive taxation, prosperous trade and the sale of church property.

4. Media - Parliament passed the Act of Supremacy in 1534, which made the King head of the church. Thus, England was able to convey her message to the masses through an expansive and most persuasive medium.

5. Manpower - England's population increased tremendously, giving her the abundance of disposable personnel needed to pursue world exploration and colonization.

America grew from a small acorn of interest into the world's biggest oak tree.

CHAPTER 10

BEFORE THE CONSTITUTION

*I*n the first incursion of Europeans into North America, eleventh century Vikings came by sea. However, they were unable to sustain their settlement in Newfoundland. Thereafter, in 1492, Spaniard Christopher Columbus and his crew sailed East in search of India.

After seventy days at sea they landed on an island Columbus called San Salvador, which is now a district of the Bahamas. Columbus had reached the Americas, east of Florida, but believed he was in the Indies. Therefore, Columbus called the inhabitants "Indians."

On the heels of Columbus' successful sortie, French, Dutch and British traders made a beeline to North America. They were purportedly seeking trade opportunities. However, that cadre of Europeans knew the inherent value of the land. Using advanced technology, communication and weapons that second wave of settlers was able to successfully dominate the people of the Americas, and establish colonies.

The Native Americans welcomed their new trading partners. The different tribal Chiefs invited them into their villages. The tribes taught them their various languages and allowed them to smoke herbs from their peace pipes.

As those traders traveled from village to village they exposed the indigenous people to measles and chicken pox. Those diseases were rarely fatal to Europeans, but almost always fatal to Native Americans. The reckless spread of these deadly diseases, including smallpox, was tantamount to genocide.

After a hundred and thirty years of enduring pestilence, sixty percent of the Native American population that lived in North America prior to the arrival of Christopher Columbus had been eradicated by disease. Those Native Americans that did not succumb to disease were brutally massacred in village raids and wars. A Native American's bow and arrow, was no match for a French or British settler's firearm.

Beginning in 1620, rather than execute convicts England transported them to North America to do her dirty work. Many of them became Indentured Servants. According to negotiated Certificates of Indenture, such "free" servants labored for a specified period of time, in exchange for their transportation, food, clothing, shelter and supplies. In the meantime, those criminals made up the forces that conquered Native Americans.

Though weak and weary, we are not done.
We dare not quit until the battle is won.

CHAPTER 11

MAKING OF A SLAVE MACHINE

I am only four generations removed from African people, who were snatched, shackled, chained and packed, like sardines, into the belly of squalid slave ships bound for the Americas. Many were strong Africans warriors who, for centuries, had defended their villages against predators. Those warriors were taken prisoner in tribal conflicts or trapped by other Africans.

No army of Portuguese, Dutch, or copycat Europeans, even if armed with guns and explosives, could have ravaged that entire continent without assistance. In exchange for mere ornaments or other goods, trusted village leaders sold righteous fathers and dutiful mothers into captivity. Those pillars of the African community did not deserve this fate or betrayal.

Each episode began when cargo ships were loaded with trade goods and launched from Europe. Upon docking on the continent of Africa, the ship's captain traded those goods for African captives. Now deemed a "Slave Ship," that vessel headed west. Upon arrival in America, the ship

44

captain traded the African captives for sugar, tobacco, and other products. Those cargo ships then returned to Europe, only to repeat the cycle.

The middle portion, or "Slave Ship portion," of this triangular trade voyage became known as the "Middle Passage." The twelve million survivors of the documented 54,000 Middle Passage voyages were dispersed throughout the United States, Canada, South America and Mexico. Although the original ancestors of all humans migrated from Africa, the American slave trade was the most significant African Diaspora – *"relocation of people of African descent."*

Considered in 1619 to be Indentured Servants, nineteen Africans were offloaded from the Dutch man of war, which docked in Jamestown, Virginia. However, in 1641 Massachusetts became the first state to recognize the race-based institution termed "Chattel Slavery." All Africans in America were classified as "unfree" laborers.

By 1654 American law classified all such "unfree" human beings as mere property and made it illegal for them to develop a family or even learn to read. White people were permitted to own them and use brute force to compel them to work without wages. Under color of law, this entire race of people was subjected to atrocious physical and psychological abuses calculated to systematically dehumanize and control them.

Some say, every war ever waged was waged over land. Land value is based upon its proximity to large bodies of water. Water may only be refreshment to some; but to traders it's the key to wealth.

CHAPTER 12

NORTH AMERICAN COLONIZATION

Spanish Conquistadors were virtually uncontested in their colonization of Cuba, Central America, Florida, the Philippines and portions of South America. Like tricky magicians, they brought forth amazing fabrics, trinkets, spices and foods. The indigenous people were awed and impressed. The chosen local trade partners parlayed their wealth into leadership. They were indebted to the Conquistadors, and did not bite the hand that fed them.

The Spaniards colonized Mexico during the sixteenth century. In 1598 Mexicans migrated to New Mexico and, in 1610, they founded the city of Santa Fe. During the Pueblo Revolt of 1680 the Mexicans banished the Spanish overseers and exercised some semblance of independent governance. In 1692, the Spaniards reestablished their authority therein.

-1-

COLONIZATION BY COALITION

The French, Dutch, and English arduously fought for command of colonies in Southern Lake Champlain, the Chesapeake Bay and along the Eastern Seaboard. It was a crafty battle of misdirection, deception and "coalitions of convenience." A Coalition of Convenience is *"a concerted effort by parties despite their divergent opinions relative to approach or overall objective."*

Parties to a coalition of convenience may be likened to public transit riders whose combined fares finance the administration and infrastructure. Yet, each rider is free to get off at any stop. By their very nature, such short-term alliances are fleeting and highly unreliable.

England and Scotland united in 1707 and became known as Britain. Strengthened as a result of this coalition, Britain was able to defeat the Dutch for control of New Amsterdam, which later became known as New York City. The British then manipulated the Iroquois to have them oppose French expansionism into Lake Champlain. As they engaged in various hostilities from 1703 until 1748, the British, French and Iroquois frequently formed and dissolved varied coalitions of convenience.

A team of rookies stepped into the big leagues. No one gave them Yankees much of a chance against them Brits, but that's the stuff that dreams are made of.

CHAPTER 13

THIRTEEN COLONIES UNITED

The original thirteen Colonial States included, Connecticut, Delaware, Georgia, Maryland, Massachusetts, New Hampshire, New York, New Jersey, North Carolina, Pennsylvania, Rhode Island, South Carolina and Virginia.

Beginning in 1756, the Seven-year war featured the Colonial States and the British, versus the Native Americans and the French. After many brutal skirmishes, the British drove the French out of the Lake Champlain region and into Canada. Their Treaty of Paris, signed in 1763, formally ended French colonization in America.

-1-

THE TOWNSHEND ACT

The seven-year war had left Great Britain in debt. Additionally, the mounting cost of defending the colonies was almost too much for the British

Empire to bear. To relieve that burden, the British Parliament passed the Townshend Act, which raised existing taxes and imposed new taxes on American colonist. Referencing their lack of a single vote in Parliament, colonist decried this as taxation without representation.

Tensions mounted as colonial protesters defiantly took to the streets. On March 5, 1770, in what later became known as the Boston Massacre, British troops gunned down five American colonists. Crispus Attakus, an African American, was the first to die for the cause of the Revolution.

Thereafter, each side engaged in a series of retaliatory actions. The colonists waged the Boston Tea Party protest of 1773 and destroyed a shipment of British tea. In response, Britain passed the 1774 Intolerable Acts, which mandated that British soldiers accused of crimes be arraigned in Britain; restricted Massachusetts Town Hall meetings; authorized the governors to take unoccupied properties to house British soldiers; and ordered the Boston port closed until the colonists reimbursed Great Britain for the tea they destroyed.

The colonists responded by forming an American Continental Congress. Establishment of this home rule governing body was the first real indication of how serious they were. The conflict had become real.

-2-

AMERICAN RESISTANCE

The American Continental Congress of the United States of America convened in 1774 as the national decision making body. With the exception of Georgia, each of the thirteen States sent representatives. Georgia did not participate because they were facing a battle against the Creek Tribe and would need the support of British troops. By resolution, the colonies petitioned Britain for redress and established the Continental Association, which prohibited the importation of British products.

John Hancock was President of the Second Continental Congress, which met from May 10, 1775 to March 1, 1781. By the time he put his ostentatious signature on the July 4, 1776 Declaration of Independence, Britain had dumped Fifty thousand convicts on American soil. As strife with the colonies intensified, Britain stopped deporting convicts to America. They feared those undesirables would join the battle against British troops.

-3-

REVOLUTIONARIES SCORE

The Revolutionary war began in 1775, when the redcoats of Great Britain attacked the colonial militia of America at Lexington and Concord. All thirteen colonies sent troops to defeat the British Regulars. That battle, teeming with death and disappointment for the British, was a confidence builder and morale booster for the colonists. In June of 1775, the colonists again defeated the British in the Battle of Bunker Hill.

In 1777, the Second Continental Congress of the United States of America adopted the nation's first governing decree. It was entitled The Articles of Confederation. A Confederation is *"a union between States, which allows each State to retain its sovereignty and any rights and powers it has not expressly delegated to the federation."*

A Federation is *"the central body that manages the cooperative efforts of governments that have formed a union."* For example, the United Nations is a federation of countries. Federation is the form of government preferred by those who advocate States Rights, like the controversial right to fly the Confederate flag.

France provided the colonies with financial assistance, weapons, ammunition and troops during the 1781 battle of Yorktown. The colonies won that battle, which ostensibly ended the war. However, the hostilities did not completely cease until the colonies and Great Britain signed the Paris Peace Treaty of 1783. "Who woulda' thunk, it?" Those rookie revolutionaries scored a major victory, the first time out.

-4-

RECOGNITION OF TRIBES

Native Americans actively supported the British in the Revolutionary War. They did so hoping to halt colonist expansion onto their lands. After the colonists won the War, they attempted to treat the Native Americans as conquered people who had forfeited the right to their land. This attempt failed.

The westward expansion of the United States resulted in the adoption of an "Indian Removal" policy, which along with its concomitant treaties forced the Native Americans from the East to areas west of the Mississippi River. Those Native Americans would later be forced to live on Reservations.

The Bureau of Indian Affairs sought to assimilate the Native Americans into mainstream society. They tried to strip them of their culture, make them more civilized and more European like. When their many attempts at religious and educational indoctrination, failed, the United States Federal government agreed to recognize the various Native American tribes as domestic dependent nations.

Tribes might achieve recognition because of their status as a political entity, by Executive Order, by treaty or statute. The factors for recognition include, continuous existence since 1900; existence as a distinct prehistoric community; and some leadership with political influence over its members. To date 561 tribes have been recognized. Each is empowered to do all things a State may do including create and enforce laws, tax, license, as well as develop, zone and manage land. Yet, the tribes cannot coin money or make war.

With the passage of the Wheeler-Howard Act of 1943, also known as the Indian Reorganization Act, Congress guaranteed Native Americans and Native Alaskans some air of sovereignty. The Act provided that these indigenous people could form businesses and associations; establish their own credit system; exercise home rule; establish vocational education; and conserve and develop the 55.7 million acres of land known as "Indian land."

Still, the United States Department of the Interior Bureau of Indian Affairs is ultimately responsible for the management and administration of that land, held in Trust by the United States.

Any reference to the Founding Fathers in terms that infer nobility would be incredibly slapdash, and should be viewed with a jaundiced eye.

CHAPTER 14

NEW NATION, OLD HABITS

Delegates to the Constitutional Convention assembled in Philadelphia during the summer of 1787. On behalf of the people of their respective colonies, they debated a lot of contentious issues. However, there was none more contentious than the issue of Slavery.

This fresh new nation had the opportunity to right the wrongs stemming from that inhumane institution, but balked. The American people had a chance to bestow citizenship upon African Americans and ensure human equality. Instead, convention delegates chose the path of least resistance.

Delegate George Mason, a Virginia planter who ultimately refused to sign the Constitution, attacked Slavery from all angles. Mason argued,

> "Slavery produces the most pernicious effect on manners. Every master of slaves is born a petty tyrant.... Slavery discourages arts and manufactures. The poor despise labor when

54

they see it performed by slaves.... I hold it
essential ... that the general government
should have the power to prevent the increase
of slavery."

Northerner Alexander Hamilton, an Antislavery
society member, did not take advantage of the
opportunity to insist on the abolishment of
Slavery. He capitulated because he feared a
disagreement over the issue of Slavery might
permanently divide the States.

Pro-slavery delegates admitted that Slavery was
an evil institution but justified its continuance on
the basis that the South's economy would
collapse without it. Southerners George
Washington and James Madison, both staunch
opponents of Slavery, also sensed a split was
imminent. Both acquiesced and joined the
delegates who arranged to sanction the institution,
without ever mentioning the term Slavery in the
Constitution.

Delegates agreed that African Americans would
be counted as three-fifths of a person for Census
purposes; decreed that fugitive slaves, who
sought refuge by crossing state lines, would be
returned to their owners; and established the year
1808, twenty years beyond ratification, as the
deadline for ending the slave trade.

The Constitution established two Houses of
Congress. The United States House of

Representatives and The United States Senate. These representatives, selected by the "People," were authorized to Tax, Legislate, Coin Money, Borrow Money, Regulate Commerce, Declare War, Raise a Military, Appropriate, and Propose and adopt amendments to the Constitution. The Senate alone was authorized to Confirm Appointments and Ratify Treaties.

Delegates to the Constitutional Convention adopted The United States Constitution on September 17, 1787. The Preamble to the Constitution affirmed,

> "We the People of the United States, in order to form a more perfect Union, establish Justice, insure domestic Tranquility, provide for the common defence, promote the general Welfare, and secure the Blessings of Liberty to ourselves and our Posterity, do ordain and establish this Constitution for the United States of America."

-1-

RATIFICATION

Constitutional Convention delegates mandated that before the Constitution could take effect as adopted, it had to be ratified by at least nine of the thirteen states. James Madison campaigned for ratification. He wrote a series of essays, which were included amongst the Federalist Papers. The tenth essay dealt with what he called "factions."

In that essay, Madison expressed great concern that "factions" might invalidate the rights of the people state-by-state. Factions are the equivalence of modern day "special interest" groups. Madison's contention was that a large Republic, not the individual States, would be better able to fend off the encroachment of faction's. In hindsight, this was the most prophetic of all arguments in favor of ratification.

Each state held a separate Ratification Convention. The substantive debate, or lack thereof in the case of Slavery, mirrored the debate in Philadelphia. Eventually, a majority of representatives, on behalf of the people of those states, voted to ratify the Constitution of the United States of America.

-2-

ELECTIONS AND ADJUSTMENTS

America was not a monarchy and would not be ruled by kings, queens, or political leaders with a birthright. The representatives of the people of the various states elected George Washington the first President of the United States of America. He was sworn in on April 30, 1789. John Adams was elected to serve as Vice President.

The first ten amendments to the Constitution, which collectively comprise the Bill of Rights, were ratified on December 15, 1791. The

Constitution has since been amended 17 times. Those amendments address various matters including Women's Suffrage, Prohibition of liquor, a subsequent repeal of the Prohibition amendment, and the allotment of Presidential Election votes for the District of Columbia.

-3-

FOUNDING FATHERS

Even before there was the concept of an America, a multitude of people came to this land for different reasons. They had their own dreams and ideas. The first European settlers to arrive in Virginia in 1607 named the area Jamestown after King of England James. This suggests they remained English loyalist.

Conversely, the Pilgrim religious congregation left England to achieve complete separation from the Church of England. In 1620, these pilgrim missionaries established their settlement in Massachusetts. They did not name their locale in honor of England's royalty, but after Plymouth - a prosperous Southwest England seaport.

The Founding Fathers were not direct descendents of Aristocrats, or in the bloodlines of any of the nearly 7,000 wealthy families with hereditary titles. They were not noble like the Rothschilds, or members of the Upper crust.

58

They had no political pedigree. They were not descendent from members of the British Parliament or any distinguished European chamber of Government. Yet, neither were they working class individuals.

These American leaders were White male, land-owning and slave-owning businessmen. They embodied many of the faults that distinguished the British Aristocracy. Consequently, they provided the American people some rights and assurances, but decidedly protected the interest of the rich.

As it was then, modern America is typically portrayed as the defender of democracy and the ultimate purveyor of all that is true and right and good. The American Spin Machine responsible for this imagery is comprised of Radio and Television networks, Newspapers, Magazines, Textbooks, and Filmmakers.

America's positive imaging was assured when on November 2, 1920, the Secretary of Commerce first granted broadcast licenses exclusively to White male applicants. The initial lack of diversity in media ownership ensured the promotion and acceptance of homogenous perspectives. It also fostered a culture where the truth often gave way to patriotic expediency.

"I could have freed more of them had they known they were slaves."

Harriet Tubman

CHAPTER 15

BREAKING OF AN AMERICAN SLAVE MACHINE

*I*n the 1856 Dred Scott decision, the United States Supreme Court declared the Negro had no rights, which the White man was bound to respect. It was officially open season on all Negros. Hundreds of thousands of African Americans were beaten, raped, crippled, castrated and killed, and there was nothing anyone could do about it. Unequivocally, the enslavement of Africans in America is the world's most despicable manifestation of man's inhumanity towards man.

American Slavery wasn't simply the ultimate power trip; it was a beloved machine that provided an economic windfall to the Southern "tobacco culture" states. Slavery made cotton picking and other labor intensive agricultrial industries prosperous.

African Americans alone were powerless to end Slavery. Multiple groups with divergent opinions formed alliances. Those overwhelming coalitions of convenience ultimately led to the cave-in of that once powerful institution.

Abolitionists wanted a complete end to slavery based upon humanitarian principles. Free-soilers believed Negroes were inferior, but opposed the expansion of slavery. Working class whites in northern industrial states opposed slavery because it replaced white workers. Despite their divergent objectives, these coalition partners were on the same train, moving in the same direction. Each could get off at any stop.

Their success was demonstrative of the effectiveness of coalitions of convenience. No one was required to compromise the principles for which they stood. They were free to participate in the effort when, where and to the extent of their chosing. The coalition partners, like members of a relay team, ran their leg and then passed the baton.

-1-

ELEMENTS OF EMANCIPATION

Several monumental elements had to manifest themselves before the American Slave Machine could finally be dismantled. Those elements included the Underground Railroad; a Civil War; Suspension of the Constitution; the Emancipation Proclamation and a Constitutional Amendment.

The Underground Railroad wasn't a mechanical railroad, but an elaborate network of safe houses and people who moved 100,000 slaves from the deep South to the North and Canada, to secure their freedom. Whether at the beginning of the mission in 1787 or at its end in 1865, sheltering and transporting slaves was risky business. However, Quaker Levi Coffin, abolitionist Harriet Tubman and John Fairfield, a White conductor who gave his life for the cause, knew the reward was worth the risk. This renegade system helped to weaken the Slave Machine.

The American Civil War, also known as the "War Between The States," began in 1861 soon after seven Southern states were denied permission to secede from the Union. The first shots were fired by the Confederate army soilders who attacked Fort Sumpter, which flew the American flag. 620,000 soldiers had been killed by the time Confederate General Robert E. Lee surrendered to Union General Ulysses S. Grant, at the Courthouse in Appomattox, Virginia, in 1865.

At the start of the Civil War, Abraham Lincoln, the newly elected 16th President of the United States, imposed martial law in territories where resistance to the North's military power might imperil the war effort. While Congress was on recess, Lincoln ordered the arrest of 13,000 Copperhead Democrats; assumed all power not expressely delegated in the Constitution and suspended habeas corpus.

Push came to shove when Chief Justice of the Supreme Court Roger Taney issued a writ of habeas corpus directing the United States military to bring prisoner John Merryman before the court. President Lincoln ordered General Cadwallader to contemptuously ignore Chief Justice Taney's directive. When considered in totality, Lincoln's aggressive actions give credence to allegations that he temporarily suspended the U.S. Constitution.

The Emancipation Proclamation of 1863 purported to free the slaves in states that had seceded from the Union. However, the Thirteenth Amendment to the Constitution, ratified in 1865, actually freed all four million African American slaves.

Many African Americans were still enslaved on June 19, 1865, when Union General Gordon Granger arrived into Galveston, Texas to inform them that the Civil War had long since ended. The Confederate Army was predominant in that part of the nation, so the inhabitants ignored Lincoln's dictates.

In honor of that day of independence, African Americans in many states celebrate a holiday called Juneteenth, which is an abbreviation for June 19th.

-2-

FIVE STAGES OF SLAVERY ABOLITION

1. Management – The Society for the Abolition of the Slave Trade. A coalition comprised of abolitionist organizations that desired a partial, if not complete, end to slavery.

2. Message - Slavery is detrimental to America's interests.

3. Money - Donations from sympathizers; Passing of collection plate at rallies; plus Profits from anti-slavery publications and paraphernalia.

4. Media - Abolitionist newspapers and anti-slavery books, abolitionist prints, posters and pamphlets, and organized lecture tours in numerous towns and cities.

5. Manpower – Working class northern Whites who were convinced that Slavery was inhumane and against their economic interests manned the Underground Railroad and the Union Army.

Now you see equality, now you don't.

CHAPTER 16

RECONSTRUCTION

Despite the several illustrious corrections, which in combination culminated in the abolition of Slavery, the United States Constitution offered African Americans no protections and no rights. The Fourteenth Amendment, passed in 1868, not only conferred citizenship upon African Americans, but also included Due Process and Equal Protection clauses that effectively nullified the holding in the Dred Scott decision. Finally, the Fifteenth Amendment, which was ratified in 1870, eliminated race based voting qualifications.

The American Racial Divide was deeper than anything anyone could imagine. Even with these additional amendments, the post slavery promise of equality was illusory. Most Whites picked at old war wounds and would not allow them to heal. They undermined every measure with the potential to empower African Americans.

During the brief Reconstruction period, which began in 1865, the United States afforded African Americans equal rights under the law; including limited educational opportunity and the right to vote. African Americans, who constituted the majority in many Southern states, effectively used their right to vote and elected many of their own to State and National government offices. Whites perceived this manipulation of the Electoral Process to be a direct threat to the balance of power, which traditionally favored them.

The unwelcomed potential for African American self-determination inspired the Tilden-Hayes compromise of 1877. This agreement to resolve the deadlocked Presidential election, resulted in the removal of Federal troops from southern states. Without that troop intervention, African Americans were powerless to exercise their Constitutional right to vote or pursue economic parity. African Americans were devastated by the immediate reversal of the social, political and economic gains they had achieved during Reconstruction.

-1-

BLACK WALL STREET

After the Civil War the state of Oklahoma freed its slaves and provided them 40 acres. Many Oklahoma towns used Restrictive Covenants to prevent African Americans from settling in White areas. Thus, Oklahoma had a number of towns populated almost exclusively by African Americans and Native Americans. The racial barrier forced segregation and resulted in the closed circulation of African American capital.

The net result was a robust African American Business District.

The center of African American business in North Tulsa, Oklahoma, was Greenwood Avenue, also known as "Black Wall Street." African Americans in North Tulsa were extremely wealthy and totally self-sufficient. They had 2 major newspapers, quality schools, a hospital, an independent bus line, hotels, a library, restaurants, nightclubs and fancy homes.

In 1901, oil was discovered four miles west of the Arkansas River at Red Fork, Oklahoma. By 1907, the Glenn Pool was the richest oil well in the nation, and Tulsa became the "Oil capital of the world." By 1920, Tulsa's population had grown from 7,298 to 70,000. Tulsa oil barons cheated the Native Americans out of their land.

Unfortunately, during the two-day 1921 race riot whites killed as many as 300 African Americans and burned Black Wall Street to the ground. For Tulsa's social climbers and oil rich titans, membership in the Ku Klux Klan, *a white supremacy group that used violence and threats to oppress African Americans*, was almost mandatory. Some say, "If they do one, they'll do two." After destroying the Greenwood Avenue business district, the ruthless oil rich began to tear down the homes of poorer white Tulsans in order to build bigger mansions.

All of the Ills, Idiosyncrasies, and Dysfunctional Attributes prevalent in African Americans are directly attributable to Slavery, Jim Crow and Economic Deprivation.

CHAPTER 17

JIM CROW

I am a vestige of the last generation of African Americans whose great-grandparents and grandparents lived the majority of their adult lives without constitutional protections or guarantees. My ancestors lived stressful lives. They were considered to be old by the time they were fifty. Their life expectancy was less than sixty years, which was far less than that of their White counter-parts.

My grandfather worked hard for the railroad. And even when he was old and gray, White people, young and old, called him "boy." Still, he found the grit to sing sweet songs, as he labored and served others, all the days of his life.

Post Reconstruction, the prevailing law of the land mandated Racial Segregation. Those so-called 'Jim Crow laws" prohibited African Americans from eating in restaurants or sleeping in most motels. They even forbade them from entering a Caucasian's home or business through the front door. Although dogs could drink water from fountains labeled "White only", my honorable great-grandparents never could.

In the 1896 Plessy v. Ferguson landmark decision, the United States Supreme Court confirmed the constitutionality of edicts mandating separate but equal accommodations.

When World War I concluded in 1918, White soldiers returned home to find that African Americans, who migrated north, occupied most of the factory jobs they had left behind. Many could not contain their resentment. From 1919 to 1921, a rash of race riots overwhelmed several major U.S. cities. Unruly White mobs, often aided and abetted by the government, viciously attacked African American workers. Clearly, the war to end all wars had not ended the race war.

In the late 1930's and early 1940's, there was persistent international strife. Japan, Italy, Germany and the Soviet Union were engaging in belligerent foreign policies. On December 7, 1941, Japan attacked Pearl Harbor and America became embroiled in World War II. American patriotism was at a fever pitch as our soldiers fought a battle of epic proportions, to stop the spread of fascism.

On February 19, 1942, in an environment of hysteria, President Franklin Delano Roosevelt signed Executive Order 9066, which ordered the internment of 120,000 Japanese and Japanese Americans. In 1944, the United States Supreme Court in Korematsu v. the United States upheld the constitutionality of the exclusion, removal and detention of Japanese Americans. That court held that the government may curtail the civil rights of any racial group when there is a "pressing public necessity." This legal principle has not been overturned.

Even while we were a nation at war, America was an especially dangerous place for African Americans. Contaminated with pervasive hatred and racially motivated ill will, White lynch mobs routinely attacked and killed African Americans with impunity.

The racist contempt for African Americans permeated every American institution, including the military. African American volunteers eager to demonstrate their loyalty and commitment to America were often untrained and inadequately equipped. They were relegated to service in segregated units.

Holocaustic Nazi prisoners of war could ride in railroad cars with White American troops; but decorated African American soldiers could not.

The stockpiling of nuclear weapons in preparation for some futuristic Star Wars is neither cost effective nor smart. In fact, it's the most ridiculous proposition man has ever conceived.

CHAPTER 18

ATOMIC AGE

The Manhattan Project, staffed by an international development team operating within the United States, resulted in the first nuclear bomb. The Plutonium bomb, which used fission to initiate the primary explosion, was successfully detonated at New Mexico test site on July 16, 1945. This event signified the beginning of the Atomic Age.

The United States dropped an Enriched Uranium bomb over Hiroshima Japan, on August 6, 1945. The detonation of this deadly device, code named "Little Boy," was followed three days later by the explosion of another Plutonium device, code named "Fat Man," over Nagasaki, Japan. These two bombs combined killed an estimated 240,000 Japanese people instantly. Thousands of others later died from the effects of radiation exposure.

These are the only times any nation has used a Nuclear bomb against an adversary. Many believe they were "Parting Shots," intended to punish Japan in retaliation for the bombing of Pearl Harbor.

After careful deliberation, Hiroshima and Nagasaki were strategically targeted to achieve maximum results. The United States wanted to clearly demonstrate it's nuclear capability to the rest of the world, as well as its willingness to use it.

Six days after the bombing of Nagasaki, Japan surrendered to the United States and the Allied Forces. This effectively ended World War II.

The U.S. and Russia went from being triumphant allies in World War II, to bitter enemies with enough military might to blow up the world 10 times over. Via high tech spy satellites circling the Earth, our genius leaders could watch the world explode in Technicolor.

CHAPTER 19

COLD WAR MEETS JIM CROW

World War II was followed by an often-edgy International cold war. Both the United States and Russia had developed deadlier Nuclear weapons, which used fusion instead of fission. Each had developed the weaponry to instantly deliver those spectacular bombs inter-continentally. Although, these two nations adopted mutual deterrent policies, their national philosophies were wholly different and politically they had little in common. Thus, the peace between them, at best, was tentative and unpredictable.

While White Americans worried that the Russians might invade our shores, strip of us our freedoms and terrorize us; African Americans were being terrorized by the cruelties of Jim Crow, Racial Segregation, the beatings, lynchings and horrific church bombings.

While Whites routinely went to bed afraid that the commies were coming; African Americans went to bed in fear of being roused in the still of the night, dragged from their homes and hung from trees, by the Ku Klux Klan.

My parents and their generational peers, African Americans born in the late 1930's and early 1940, were the children of Christians who sought to love their neighbors as they loved themselves. These loyal patriots loved an America that did not love them back. Members of that younger generation grew up perplexed and with mixed emotions.

African American children, naïve to the peculiarities of the Jim Crow South, were often at risk. When my father was eight years of age he refused to coward to a White man in a Memphis, Tennessee grocery store. My grandparents feared the White man would make good on his promise to retaliate. So like many other families who migrated north during that period, they left town; not for economic reasons but to escape the threat of violence.

America offered African Americans no protection from White hate mongers emboldened by Jim Crow laws. The best hope for the survival of African American children rested in virtual invisibility. The philosophy was, "they can't hit, what they can't see."

Therefore, the compliant community indoctrinated their children with universal rules of survival. They taught them to be Jim Crow law-abiding, polite, respectful of adults, and to avoid making eye contact with Whites.

It may be difficult for some people to understand the real effect this intimidation had on future generations of African Americans. But, as one who grew up in the midst of people who believed they were limited in ability, I assure you, the effect is real.

I've heard people say, "Slavery ended in 1865, you weren't even born yet. Surely you can't blame slavery for your problems today." Those people don't understand that the physical and mental anguish did not end with slavery. Jim Crow, which only officially ended in 1965, though not as physically abusive, may have been more emotionally damaging.

Slaves could prepare their mindset to endure their everyday debilitating circumstances. Slaves had no expectation of protection. Thus, there was no let down or disappointment when officials failed to snatch the whip from the master's hand. However, there is nothing that could ward off the frustration of a free African American who is disappointed when the Calvary shows up and joins the lynch mob. Such a betrayal was more likely than not to induce a Post Traumatic Stress Syndrome, with lasting negative affects.

The civil rights movement was launched to inject fairness into every essence, fiber, and milieu of our society.

CHAPTER 20

MODERN CIVIL RIGHTS MOVEMENT

*I*n late August of 1955, fourteen-year-old Chicagoan Emmett Till was brutally murdered in Money, Mississippi for, supposedly, whistling at a White woman. The modern day Civil Rights movement began in earnest when Mamie Till-Mobley, who wanted to reveal what they had done to her child, insisted on an open casket funeral.

Arguably, the sight of that child's mutilated body shocked the consciousness of African Americans. Once and for all, they realized they had to do more than simply wait for the sick racist system that threatened their children to heal itself.

The modern Civil Rights Movement had impetus but needed a cause that would touch the hearts and souls of African Americans. Certainly, the movement would have to grow to include everyone. But it had to begin in the affected community.

For years E.D. Nixon President of the Alabama NAACP had fought, inch by inch, for justice in Montgomery. E.D. was the epitome of a leader. Immediately upon hearing that Rosa Parks had been arrested for refusing to give up her seat on the bus, so that a White man could sit in the Colored only row, E.D. sprung into action. He posted Ms. Park's bail, and then recruited her to be the subject of the effort to confront the practice of Racial Segregation on Montgomery city buses.

Armed with momentum and a universal cause, the Civil Rights Movement now needed a visionary to galvanize the masses. A visionary is *"a leader endowed with the ability to see beyond the ordinary; hone that foresight into a skill; and actively advance a campaign from its obvious conception to its unimaginable conclusion."*

E.D. Nixon hastily convened a meeting of local preachers to organize a one-day Montgomery bus boycott. At that meeting preachers who knew the viciousness of Montgomery segregationist vacillated. E.D. threatened to tell everyone in town that they were too cowardly to boycott.

-1-

KING'S FIRST STAND

The new pastor of the Dexter Avenue Baptist Church, Reverend Dr. Martin Luther King, Jr., seized the moment and rose to adamantly distinguish himself from any cowards in the group. The congregation of preachers promptly elected. Dr. King President of the newly formed Montgomery Improvement Association.

Leadership is not limited to any one individual. Many people are leaders in their own right. However, no one is the leader of all causes all of the time. Preachers serve as the leaders of their church and parishioners. However, under certain circumstances, they may be required to serve as supporters.

Reverend Dr. King walked into the meeting as a simple supporter of the Montgomery bus boycott organizing effort. He stood and was recognized as a leader amongst leaders. King emerged with the opportunity to prove that he was a visionary.

On December 5, 1955, ninety percent of the African American ridership boycotted city buses. Volunteers, private employers and cabs provided rides for people seeking to get to school or work. The visionary Dr. King looked beyond this local success, and saw the opportunity to bring justice to African American bus riders everywhere.

That evening, at Holt Street Church Dr. King rallied several thousand supporters with his courage, inspirational tone and analytical insight. The Montgomery Improvement Association under his leadership presented a Resolution that outlined the offense, described its affect, and authorized a boycott as the remedy. The supporters voted unanimously to continue the boycott until the city agreed to meet their desegregation demands.

Despite harassment, intimidation, threats, arrests, and house bombings, the Montgomery bus boycotters remained resolute. On November 13, 1956, The United States Supreme Court ruled Alabama's bus Segregation laws unconstitutional. The Montgomery bus boycott officially ended on December 21, 1956, after the city passed an ordinance permitting African Americans to sit anywhere on buses, without discrimination.

-2-

FIVE STAGE MONTGOMERY BUS BOYCOTT

1. Management - the formation of the Montgomery Improvement Association.
2. Message – African Americans won't ride the bus until they are treated as equals.
3. Money – Sunday collection plate offerings and passing of the hat at the Holt Street Church rally.
4. Media – Television and Newspaper coverage of the meeting at Holt Street Church. Organizers distributed, to all other media sources, copies of the official Resolution that outlined the offense, its affect and a declaration of the boycott.
5. Manpower – Volunteers, including cabs and employers, provided rides for boycotters.

Camelot was the fictional castle from which King Arthur ruled all that he surveyed. He and his court of brave and noble knights fought for truth and justice.

CHAPTER 21

CAMELOT

I was born in 1957; three years after the U. S. Supreme Court's Brown v. Board of Education decision overturned the separate but equal doctrine; and three years before the election of John F. Kennedy, as the first Roman Catholic President of the United States. Kennedy's eloquent speeches inspired Americans to act Nationally, think Globally, and dream Intergalactically.

John F. Kennedy was young, charismatic, and wholesome. The television cameras fell in love with his wife Jacqueline and their two children. The dignified and regal imagery surrounding this attractive family earned the moniker "Camelot."

The Democrat Party was transitioning from the party of bigotry, into the party of social tolerance. As a Senator, it was politically expedient for John Kennedy to vote against the 1957 Civil Rights Act proposed to Congress by Republican President Dwight Eisenhower. However, as he campaigned for the Presidency, Kennedy made clear his support of Civil Rights.

Although not a political monolith, African Americans often vote as one. Members of this diverse racial group share core values and ideals. Despite party affiliation and history, Jack Kennedy (in the Irish vernacular men named John are called Jack) was seen as capable and willing to address the vital interests of African Americans. Consequently, Kennedy received a substantial percentage of the African American vote.

Robert J. Kennedy served as Attorney General during the presidency of his older brother John. He was most committed to bringing mafia members to justice. One highlight of his career was the televised hearings during which he grilled Union boss Jimmy Hoffa, concerning alleged financial corruption and electoral misconduct.

Although, Attorney General Robert Kennedy issued a directive to the FBI authorizing them to wiretap Dr. King in 1961, he too was a strong proponent of Civil Rights. Bobby is credited with encouraging President Kennedy to aggressively pursue Civil Rights legislation. In that arena, the Kennedy's had their hands full as the roar for improved race relations in America grew deafening.

Let's not focus on the hate filled people who did hateful things. Let's concentrate on the heroes who rose from obscurity to preserve our faith in humanity.

CHAPTER 22

RACIAL UNREST

*A*t age five I was reading the newspaper from cover to cover. I was too young to fully comprehend the degradation and shame wrought by Jim Crow laws. But I vicariously felt the pain of my community. I eagerly followed the rise of social unrest. It readily became apparent that African Americans were sick and tired of being sick and tired.

Heretofore, African Americans barely whispered as they sat around the kitchen table criticizing Whites who perpetrated injustice in America. African American dissidents whispered because of the lessons hard learned during slavery. Slaves, who huddled in the Slave quarters and criticized the Slave Master or plotted to escape, were often whipped and beaten the very next day. The Slave quarters didn't have ears; Master had snitches – *traitors who inform on others.*

Those once whispering African Americans were now taking their protests to the streets. Any

Sunday after church you might find granddad, grandma and young parents with children in tow, marching for equality. Those frustrated protesters knew they risked being violently attacked and possibly arrested. However, they also knew the system had failed them and someone had to do something. Whites, determined to maintain the status quo, lined the protest route to taunt the peaceful protestors and hurl objects at them.

At the tender age of six, I was disturbed by television news coverage featuring a hateful Theophilus Eugene "Bull" Connor, the Public Safety Commissioner of Birmingham, Alabama. Bull Connor was possibly the most bigoted man in American history. He was an avowed Segregationist who wore his racism on his sleeve. Bull Connor was one of the few proud Ku Klux Klan members, who didn't hide under a sheet.

I was indelibly impressed by television footage that, one minute, showed African American children peacefully marching for fairness and decency; and the next minute showed Bull Connor ordering his police to brutally beat them, attack them with police dogs, and spray them with water from forceful hoses.

Whites in Birmingham, who witnessed the same, repeatedly elected Bull Connor. They empowered him to do whatever was necessary to keep African Americans in their lowly place.

-1-

MARCH ON WASHINGTON

A. Phillip Randolph, President of the International Brotherhood of Sleeping Car Porters, initiated and organized the March on Washington for freedom and jobs. Randolph marshaled the support of the many labor unions. On August 28, 1963 Reverend Dr. Martin L. King, Jr. gave the keynote address

Before a crowd of 250,000 marchers, in the so-called "I have a dream speech," Rev. Dr. King promised,

"There will be neither rest nor tranquility in America until the Negro is granted his citizenship rights." However, King warned "The marvelous new militancy which has engulfed the Negro community must not lead us to distrust all white people, for many of our white brothers, as evidenced by their presence here today, have come to realize that their destiny is tied up with our destiny and their freedom is inextricably bound to our freedom."

Dr. King was ever mindful of the hazards inherent in the struggle for Civil Rights. It was his belief that the best hope for achievement of full citizenship was rooted in the non-violent course he had cautiously charted. King's movement was premised upon civil disobedience but only to the extent necessary to highlight the cruelties of the unjust American system. King exposed social contradictions and held them up in sharp relief. His movement appealed to the humanity hidden in the righteous amongst us.

However there was another movement on another track, which threatened the viability of King's coalition of willing Whites and patient African Americans. Newly emerging African American militants were not impressed by King's accomplishments. They felt America owed them more than meager successes. Their brutal diatribes and anti-white outbursts constantly tested the resolve of King's coalition partners.

-2-

THE ANTI-RACIST

Chief among the emerging militants was Malcolm X who in his inimitable fashion, referred to the March on Washington as the "Farce on Washington."

Born Malcolm Little on May 19, 1925, in Omaha, Nebraska; he was the diligent son of a Civil Rights activist murdered by White hooligans. While in prison for Grand Larceny, Little began to study the Islamic faith. He became a Muslim and changed his surname to "X." This non-descript demarcation symbolized the identity and heritage stripped from African Americans.

Malcolm X, a strong proponent of Black Nationalism, was the leader largely responsible for the rising popularity of the Nation of Islam. He was a prolific speaker who moved audiences, with empowering ideas and appeals to character. Malcolm warned against integration and contradicted the movement that urged non-violence. He was committed to the achievement of respect and dignity "By any means necessary."

King was the calm and Malcolm was the storm. King was patient and Malcolm was fervent. King was caution and Malcolm was contempt. King was moderate and Malcolm was extremist.

The Malcolm X style movement was the counter Ku Klux Klan.

-3-

WHEN THE KLAN ATTACKS

King recognized how powerless African Americans were against the institutions that perpetuated racism and inequality in America. Yet, he was aware of an increasing tide of compassion and empathy for the plight of the Negro. King was concerned that violent acts by militants could make African Americans appear undeserving of the White empathy needed to pass Civil Rights legislation.

Less than a month after the peaceful March on Washington members of the Ku Klux Klan went on the attack. They exploded nineteen sticks of dynamite outside the basement of the Sixteenth Street Baptist Church, in Birmingham, Alabama. The blast killed four young girls and injured twenty-two others. The African American community mourned.

Three days later, an arrogant and unremorseful Bull Connor retorted that the United States Supreme Court should be held responsible for those deaths. His outrageous comment was a stark reminder of how low a racist could go. Even Whites who hadn't empathized with the March on Washington were outraged by his callousness.

Racism, like oppression is real. It changes people's lives and scars them in ways that even time can't heal.

CHAPTER 23

FALL OF SEGREGATION

Camelot and its entire majestic splendor abruptly ended when President Kennedy was assassinated in Dallas, Texas, on November 22, 1963. Americans reeled at the loss of one of the most captivating and promising leaders in history. At the time of his death, President Kennedy's bold initiatives were addressing the needs of the poor and stimulating the nation's economy.

Kennedy's decisive posturing had made America seem safer from persistent Communist threats. Americans remembered that he did not blink during the Cuban Missile Crisis. That perception became his reality. President Kennedy, a strong proponent of human equality, never got the chance to sign Civil Rights legislation.

Although President Johnson was much less fascinating than Kennedy, he soon became a favorite of Civil Rights activists. In July of 1964, Johnson signed the Civil Rights Act, which prohibited segregation in schools and public places. With that legislation finally in place, on

September 3, 1964, Attorney General Robert Kennedy left the Johnson administration to campaign for election to the United States Senate.

Legal Segregation had been dealt a deathblow and was doomed to die. Business as usual was gasping for air. Unfortunately, the end of Legal Segregation was a boon for Racial Discrimination.

-1-

THE ART OF RACIAL DISCRIMINATION

The Civil Rights Act of 1964 outlawed Racial Segregation - the lawful separation of people on the basis of race. However, it had little or no effect on Racial Discrimination - the unfair or unlawful treatment of a person or persons within a protected class because of their race.

Both Legal Segregation and Racial Discrimination are fundamentally oppressive methods of denigrating African Americans. Both caused tremendous damage to the psyche. During Segregation the differences between White and Black facilities were obvious and distinct. There were objective means by which to measure the disparity between the races.

However, once African Americans were integrated into the whole of America, the disparate treatment was less obvious. Through sinister means, practiced under the radar, Whites were able to deprive African Americans of employment, education, economic assistance, healthcare, safety services, and housing.

Historically, Southerners and Northerners used divergent methods to achieve the disparate treatment of African Americans. While growing up, I often heard it said that "Southern racists will tell you to your face that you are not welcome in their neck of the woods, whereas Northern racists will throw a rock at you and hide their hand." This precept is rooted in the recognition that Southerners mainly relied on the open and notorious practice of Legal Segregation, whereas Northerners practiced Racial Discrimination, which is a covert art form.

-2-

RACISM

Desegregation forced Whites to interact with African Americans as equals. This resulted in an increase in Racism – "*the disparate treatment of people based upon their ethnic characteristics by one with the power to affect outcomes.*" Whites had the Power, *"the force strength or ability to move something, or make something happen,"* and they used it to intimidate and suppress African Americans.

My family lived in Chicago, a big city North of the Mason Dixon line. In 1966 we were the second African American family to purchase a house on the 8100 South Euclid block. Rather than welcome us, our White neighbors dumped garbage in our yard, hurled racial epithets, attempted to run us over as we rode our bikes, attacked us as we journeyed to the store or as we sat on Rainbow beach.

The Civil Rights Act forced cafeteria owners to allow African Americans to sit down and eat, but couldn't stop the racist cook from spitting in their food. The Housing Discrimination laws enabled African Americans to buy homes in White neighborhoods, but could not make racist neighbors act neighborly.

As far back as slavery, African Americans have had the power to affect Whites. Yet, they have not systematically use that power to engage in racist behavior hurtful to other human beings. The slaves who cooked the meals did not attempt to poison the slave master. The nannies did not abuse White children, but instead loved them and cared for them as though they were their own.

On the average plantation, which was usually distant and isolated, African Americans greatly outnumbered the Slave Masters and their families. There were no phones to dial 9-1-1 in the middle of the night. There was nothing to prevent these oppressed people from extracting revenge, except abiding human decency.

This was an abolitionist's most compelling argument to dispel claims that African Americans were sub-human. King was ever mindful of this as he preached nonviolence, while sitting on the powder keg of a new Black militancy.

-3-

WAR ON POVERTY

President Lyndon Baines Johnson ran for re-election in 1964. Reverend Dr. Martin Luther King, Jr. campaigned for him, something he hadn't done for John F. Kennedy. Dr. King and President Johnson were two peas in a pod. They shared common philosophies and objectives.

They formed an effective Coalition. Dr. King delivered votes; President Johnson delivered the meat and potatoes in the War on Poverty. Johnson advanced the notion that the State should operate as a safety net and provide opportunity for the most needy within our society. He was able to pass the Economic Opportunity Act of 1964, which included Medicare, Medicaid and Education Assistance.

Freshman Senator Robert J. Kennedy was often pictured in circumstances that demonstrated his personal concern for the less fortunate. Traveling throughout America Bobby Kennedy championed causes important to minorities. Among other things, he boldly pushed the Democratic Party to do more to end Racial Discrimination. Senator Kennedy was becoming more strident in his opposition to the war in Vietnam.

Kennedy was noted for his unconventional approach to International affairs. He traveled to South Africa to encourage the oppressed majority at a time when most American politicians avoided the issue of Apartheid. Predicated upon Afrikanerdom Christian doctrines, South African Apartheid was *the legal separation of the minority white Afrikaner population from the majority black and colored population.* Apartheid, established by the Dutch controlled National Party, which controlled South Africa's government in 1948, was a legacy of the British Empire.

-4-

MALCOLM AFTER MECCA

Malcolm X traveled to Jeddah, Saudi Arabia in 1964, to make the traditional Muslim Pilgrimage to Mecca. Because he was an American citizen who did not speak Arabic, he was separated from the others and his status as a Muslim was questioned.

After intervention by Saudi dignitaries, Malcolm X was allowed to complete the Hajj. He was positively impacted by the wholesome interaction of Muslims of different races. Malcolm arrived at the conclusion that racial differences could be reconciled through Islam.

Malcolm X disavowed his separatist belief and broke ties with Elijah Muhammad and the Nation of Islam. His most famous speech, "The Ballot or the Bullet" emphasized voting as a means of achieving justice in America. He suggested Blacks would do well to elect other Blacks to represent their interest. Malcolm X also underscored the importance of redirecting the energy of the movement from a struggle for Civil Rights, to one for Human Rights.

On February 21, 1965, Malcolm X, now called "el-Hajj Malik el-Shabazz," was delivering a speech from the podium of the Audubon Ballroom, in Harlem, New York. Someone yelled, *"Get your hand outta my pocket! Don't be messin' with my pockets!"*

During the ensuing commotion, three members of the Nation of Islam rushed to the podium and shot Malcolm X sixteen times. Those assailants were captured by the crowd and later convicted of his murder.

-5-

STRUGGLE FOR VOTING RIGHTS

Although the Fifteenth Amendment to the United States Constitution granted all U. S. citizens the right to vote, that right remained a States right. To prevent African Americans from registering to vote, many states required they pass literacy tests, or pay cost prohibitive poll taxes.

As a stopgap, the "Grandfather clause" made illiterate Whites eligible to register and vote if their grandfather had voted. In many states, fewer than fifty-percent of the African Americans who were eligible to vote were actually registered.

In towns all across America, streets were stained by the blood of African Americans who didn't back down when their right to vote was being denied. Even before the fresh blood was washed away there was another hardheaded uppity Negro standing at the table refusing to take no for an answer. Yet, there was never a shortage of racist enforcers eager to show them the heel of their boot, the butt of their rifle, or the end of a rope.

On March 7, 1965, six hundred men, women, and children began a 54-mile march from Selma to Montgomery. They sought to protest the police shooting of Vietnam veteran Jimmie Lee Jackson and their lack of voting rights. Although African American's were the majority of Selma's population, they were only one percent of the registered voters.

As soon as the protesters marched across the Edmund Pettis Bridge, local and State police hurled tear gas at them and beat them with nightsticks. Television networks interrupted regular programming to broadcast images of defenseless children being beaten bloody. Immediately referred to as "Bloody Sunday," this incident shocked Americans everywhere.

-6-

SAFETY FIRST, LAST AND ALWAYS

As a general rule, no matter how persuasive the leader or how noble the cause, not many civilians will willingly journey into harms way. Nevertheless, inspired by King's tenacity and infectious courage, Thousands of brave and committed sympathizers flocked to Selma to participate in a subsequent attempt at crossing the bridge, scheduled for the following Tuesday.

Among the most critical challenges faced by any leader is that of ensuring the safety of their supporters. In a culture where violence has often been employed, as a means of breaking ones will to persist or resist, safety is always the first concern. This holds true whether the effort is military or civilian, corporate or domestic.

They started out that Tuesday, twenty-five hundred strong. Dr. King had sought a court order to protect the marchers from the hostile White police and angry mobs waiting on the other side of the bridge. However, the judge had indicated he needed more time to render a decision. Rather than place the willing marchers in harms way, Dr. King led them as far as the bridge. Following a brief prayer he unexpectedly dismissed them. Although, many were disappointed that this attempted crossing was aborted, it was the safest and most sensible thing to do.

On the third try, Sunday, March 21, 1965, under the protection of Federal troops three thousand-two hundred marchers safely crossed the Edmund Pettis Bridge.

They proceeded to Montgomery, marching along the side of the road by day and sleeping in fields during the night. Their numbers swelled. Four days later, twenty-five thousand marchers arrived at the State Capitol, unscathed.

-7-

VOTING PROTECTION

Americans finally had enough of the violent police beatings of Bloody Sunday marchers and participants in similar peaceful marches. Those scandalous televised images stirred the emotions of average everyday people everywhere. They reacted in a manner, which prompted their elected representatives to take action. President Johnson collared the momentum and passed legislation designed to ensure every eligible person's ability to vote.

The Voting Rights Act was signed on August 6, 1965. It outlawed poll taxes and literacy tests, and actually provided the federal enforcement necessary to guarantee African Americans the opportunity to register and vote. Contrary to Urban Legend, the voting rights of African Americans do not periodically expire. However, certain federal voting enforcement tools do have to be reauthorized.

The Section 5 Pre-Clearance clause of the Voting Rights Act mandated that certain States receive approval prior to instituting any substantial changes to their voting practices. Additionally, the Act empowered Federal examiners to review the qualifications of potential voters, and Federal observers to monitor elections and thereby ensure the voting rights remain unimpaired. Congress reauthorized, and sitting Presidents signed, those temporary amendments along with the Section 4 bilingual interpretation provision, in years 1970, 1975, 1982 and 2006.

A man had a brother by a different father and a different mother; of a different faith and a different creed. They had similar hopes and similar needs; thus they were brothers; brothers indeed.

CHAPTER 24

KINDERED SPIRITS

*T*hroughout his public career Dr. Martin Luther King, Jr. had taken a stand on every major issue of importance to African Americans. However, he rarely stood alone. Along the way, he attracted diverse coalition partners: African Americans, Caucasians, Northerners, and Southerners; each came with their own axe to grind.

Dr. King was the catalyst most responsible for highlighting the need for Civil Right and Voting Right legislation. However, President Johnson had the relationships necessary to pass those pieces of legislation and the pen to sign them into law. Dr. King and President Johnson achieved those momentous changes through coalition.

Throughout his years of service, Dr. King's nonviolent approach was questioned by defense minded African American leaders. Among them was activist Stokley Carmichael. While just a

New York high school student, Stokley joined the Congress On Racial Equality. C.O.R.E was most notable for its Woolworth's lunch counter sit-ins. Although he marched with King nonviolently, Stokley's philosophy was more akin to that of Robert Williams, an advocate of Armed Defense, who originated the phrase "Black Power" in the late 50s.

In April of 1967, Reverend Dr. King planned to deliver a major policy statement expressing his opposition to the War in Vietnam. He phoned Stokley Carmichael and invited him to sit in the front row. Dr. King was aware that his stance would cause conflict between he and President Johnson. By extending that special invitation to a self-defense minded militant, King indicated his preparedness to transition into a new coalition.

During that speech, Dr. King demonstrated his consistency. He was nonviolent when it came to resisting Jim Crow segregationist, and equally as nonviolent when it came to resisting the international spread of communism. Despite the fact that King's logic was undeniable, many characterized his stance as unpatriotic. As expected, the King-Johnson coalition unceremoniously dissipated.

When the King-Johnson door closed, the King-Kennedy door opened. Over a period of time, Bobby Kennedy and Martin King had become close allies in the battle to end racism.

Both were opposed to the war in Vietnam. Both were fighting to advance the causes of poor people. King and Kennedy were kindred spirits. They were seatmates, with no parachutes, on a flight "from suffering to success."

-1-

TRIPLE THREAT TO STATUS QUO

In November of 1967, Dr. King introduced his Poor Peoples Campaign. His goal was to focus attention on the issues affecting the poverty stricken of all races. Having always enjoyed some modicum of multi-racial support, his organization was now demonstrating the vision necessary to broaden its scope and, thus, remain viable. King announced plans to go back to Washington for another massive protest.

Dr. King had recently expanded the work of the Southern Christian Leadership Conference. He initiated Operation Breadbasket to address economic injustices. The recently established Chicago division, under the direction of a young and aggressive Jesse Louis Jackson, successfully organized boycotts against businesses that did not offer fair employment to African Americans. Dr. King named Jackson national director of Operation Breadbasket in 1967.

On March 16, 1968, King cohort Senator Robert J. Kennedy announced his run for the Presidency of the United States of America. On March 31, 1968, President Johnson withdrew his candidacy for re-election. Vice President Hubert Humphrey then promptly entered the race.

Although other activists questioned Dr. King's nonviolent approach, he was the undisputed preeminent Civil Rights leader with an unequaled ability to inspire the masses. His Operation Breadbasket was forcing businesses to employ African Americans in meaningful positions. This was indicative of his tremendous potential to affect the economic balance in America. Additionally, King was poised to be the deciding factor in the race for the U.S. Presidency.

As a leader in the Civil Rights movement, Economic Empowerment movement and on the National Political scene, now more than ever before, Dr. King was a triple threat poised to upset the balance of power in America.

-2-

KING'S LAST STAND

The Memphis sanitation workers, on strike for increased wages and better working conditions, were hopelessly at odds with that city's Mayor. Each of their most recent marches had ended in violence. The social and political environment in Memphis was exceedingly dangerous. King's friends and advisors were leery. They expressed concern for his peaceful image as well as for his personal safety. Despite those warnings, Dr. King traveled to Memphis to stand with those working men and women, anyway.

On the evening of April 3, 1968 Dr. King, feeling a little under the weather, had decided to skip the mass meeting at the Bishop Mason Temple. He asked his best friend, Reverend Ralph Abernathy, to go and serve as his surrogate speaker. When Abernathy called Dr. King from the Temple and implored him to come and briefly speak, he hurried over.

After Abernathy's presentation, Dr. King gave a fiery extemporaneous speech. He concluded with the refrain "Mine eyes have seen the glory of the coming of the Lord." He returned from the podium, and nearly collapsed in his seat. King wept.

On the following evening, April 4 1968, Dr. King and his entourage were leaving the Lorraine Motel in Memphis Tennessee, to go have dinner at the home of a friend and supporter, Rev. Billy Kyles. While standing on the motel balcony Dr. Martin Luther King, Jr. was assassinated.

As word of his death spread, decent people everywhere wailed in pain. Many within the White Power structure celebrated and insisted it was "good riddance." A large number of African Americans echoed that sentiment.

Spontaneous riots broke out as Dr. King's sympathizers retaliated against the system that fostered the kind of hatred that allowed King to be killed. Cities all across America went up in flames as people acted upon their frustration. African Americans burned down the building and businesses in their own neighborhoods.

After years of standing up for humanity, Time Man of the Year, Nobel Peace Prize recipient, Reverend Dr. Martin Luther King, Jr. was finally laid to rest in Atlanta Georgia on April 9, 1968.

-3-

KENNEDY'S LAST STOP

The Presidential Campaign of Senator Robert Kennedy moved across America inspiring hope in throngs of Democrats. Among other things, they hoped that he would help rid America of Institutional Racism – *'the failure of a governmental, economic or publicly regulated entity to fairly consider all persons irrespective of race. "*

Arguably, Institutional Racism was the last frontier in the fight for equality in America. Insidious and almost undetectable, it was practiced in places where there were no eyewitnesses.

104

Alive and well in every state, Institutional Racism quietly factored into decisions pertaining to Employment, Banking, Financing, Education, Emergency Assistance, Healthcare, Housing Discrimination, Insurance Redlining, Police Protection, Public Prosecution, and Public Safety. Senator Kennedy targeted this stubborn American bastion which because of its covert nature, afforded offenders plausible deniability.

However, on June 5, 1968, moments after delivering his California primary victory speech, Senator Robert J. Kennedy was gunned down in the kitchen pantry adjacent to a San Francisco Ambassador Hotel Ballroom.

Once again, Americans were left to grieve. However, the Assassin's bullet did more than kill another promising leader; it ended the surge to totally eliminate Institutional Racism and protect Human Rights.

I'm the descendent of an African whom Massa' gave the nonsensical label Runaway Slave. A pejorative oxymoron, ridiculous but grave; criminalizing the brave who wouldn't stay on the plantation and behave.

CHAPTER 25

HOMELESS NAMELESS PEOPLE

*E*ven if reluctantly, most American immigrants voluntarily left their homeland. They had the opportunity to wave goodbye to loved ones, and knew that if things didn't work out, they could always return home.

When they arrived in America they were free to associate with anyone they chose. They were often comforted by friends and supported by relatives and countrymen who had arrived before them.

African Americans were brought to America by force. They were stripped of their language and their culture. They had neither the method nor means to communicate with anyone in Africa.

I can imagine slave traders delivering deceptive messages to their loved ones back home. The message was always the same: "Everything is fine. America is a beautiful place. Please get on the boat, so that you may join me at once."

African Americans who were several generations removed from the slave trade had no way to determine their place of origin. All trails had grown cold. Thus, those of African descent, born in America, were completely cut-off from all birthright and inheritances.

Early Slaves had no connection to any other Africans in America or anywhere else on the planet. We had no bona fide place to call home. African Americans had to settle for adoption of the entire continent as their 'Motherland.'

-1-

STRANGE NAMES

For years, we had no rights to rescue us from tyrannical subjugation. African Americans had no positive ethnic group characterization. Under threat of punishment we were forced to answer to anything we were called.

Even if a White man called you by the pejorative "Nigger," Jim Crow law dictated that you respond promptly and respectfully. For generations African Americans displayed great respect for unjust laws. Fortunately, the public use of this word with evil intent has greatly diminished.

I do believe we should tell children not to use the word Nigger or Nigga'. It doesn't matter how you spell it. It doesn't matter how harmless the application. It is still perceived by many to be a haunting unsociable utterance. However, I don't believe we should focus on that word any more than we would any other profane word.

Words are intangible tools. They only have the substance or power that we grant them. If we have to teach a child that they should shudder or have an emotional reaction when they hear a particular word, we are substantiating that word and giving it power over that child. We must be careful not to transfer our negative association with a simple word to yet another generation.

The power was not in the pejorative "Nigger" for a race based slur uttered by one who doesn't matter is nothing more than a rhetorical insult. The power was in the fear or intimidation it once caused.

In law, if someone took a swing at you and you didn't know it, you could not reasonably experience fear or intimidation. Thus, you were not assaulted. It does not matter what the assailant intended. The offense is dependent upon you immediately being affected by that action.

Similarly, if someone said something derogatory to you in a foreign language that you did not understand, you cannot reasonably be offended by that utterance.

All racial slurs have a limited life span. Today's younger generation, African Americans, Whites, and Latinos have begun to use the word Nigga' as a term of endearment. For most of them, it has no prejudicial or racial connotation, whatsoever. If left alone, over time, they will completely outgrow the word. If we stop focusing on that slur, once and for all, it will become obsolete.

-2-

UMGAWA, BLACK POWER

As far back as 1619, when the first African slaves arrived in America, Caucasians denoted us using various labels that were consistent only with our physical characteristics. Initially, Caucasians designated that we be called Negro, which in Spanish means black.

In 1844, near the end of slavery and during Reconstruction they referred to us as Colored. In 1877, at the start of the Jim Crow era, Caucasians returned to use of the designation Negro. Eventually, we stumbled across our own identifier.

In 1968, Stokley Carmichael breathed new life into the daring phrase "Black Power." Even today it conjures up images of pride and unity. Defiant men draped in black leather coats; the ends of their big bushy afros sticking out from the rims of black tams caps; tight bellbottom pants with a piece tucked in the waistband; standing on the corner giving dap while planning a revolution not fit for television; all eyes watching the pigs roll slowly by.

Thirteen years earlier, during his "Call to Consciousness" speech, Dr. King referred to us as "black people." In an effort to embody the essence of Black Power, we began to refer to ourselves as Black. Similar to the identifiers Caucasians had given us, this was only a characterization. However, the fact that we chose it ourselves, made it cool.

Finally, in 1997 Rev. Jesse L. Jackson successfully pushed for adoption and use of the more accurate heritage based designation: "African American."

The identifier "Black" still has relevance in the American glossary of terms. It is appropriately used as a catchall reference concerning anyone in America who appears to be of recent African descent, irrespective of place of birth. The offense of "Driving While Black" is predicated upon one's appearance, not country of origin.

Hippies were the beatniks who'd spent too much time listening to the Last Poets. They wanted to be stoned when the revolution...

CHAPTER 26

HIPPIE BREAKDOWN

*D*uring the early 1960s there were an abundance of Hippies – *"free-love activists whose main thrust was to effect social change."* Hippies were easily recognizable by their non-conforming scruffy appearances and the Volkswagen hippie mobiles they drove from concert to protest, and back again. Their movement was mostly made up of conscientious objectors who opposed the war in Vietnam and, pacifists who wanted the whole world to live in harmony.

However, the Hippie protest movement proved to be unsustainable in the aftermath of the infamous police riot at the 1968 Democratic National Convention in Chicago. Mayor Richard J. Daley said it best, "The police are not here to create disorder; they're here to preserve disorder." That shameful escapade, during which protestors were bloodied and brutalized by Chicago police, was the last hurrah for protestors of that decade.

For activists who empathized with those protesters, the danger hit too close to home. They

111

starkly realized that they too could be victimized. That reality was sobering. That uncomfortable truth robbed the hippies of their will to persist.

-1-

TOWNSHEND ACT II

Some say the Chicago police beat the snot out of the 60s protestors. Whatever the case, those pacifists were no longer willing to risk their personal well being for any cause. The 1969 Woodstock musical festival, staged in Bethel, New York, was the occasion that confirmed this paradigm shift in attitude. It was best epitomized by the incident involving famed Chicago Seven activist Abbie Hoffman.

During the Woodstock performance of The Who, Hoffman grabbed the mike and attempted to make a statement protesting the jailing of White Panther Party member John Sinclair. Guitarist Pete Townshend promptly knocked Hoffman off the stage. The Hippie crowd roared its approval. At that moment, that generation, embodied by that crowd, decreed itself divorced from social activism.

-2-

FROM CONCERTS TO CAPITALISM

By the early 1970s those once devout activists no longer protested to change the world. They morphed into capitalist. Erstwhile hippies who'd dodged the draft and couldn't risk applying for a corporate job, as well as those too nostalgic to part with their beards, began promoting concerts or marketing the paraphernalia associated with the concepts of Peace, Love and Personal Freedom.

Society witnessed the rise of the Me Attitude – *"a focus on self and immersion in the pursuit of material things."* During that era, with the exception of Vietnam War protestors, Americans did not participate in any sustained political movements.

Today, peaceful activists who seek to protect people's freedoms are still at risk of being attacked by advocates with opposing views. The struggle for abortion rights may best illustrate this hazard. Some zealots, who ironically promote the right to life, have demonstrated willingness to bomb abortion facilities and indiscriminately take the lives of innocent people. Just as in the past, a modern leader seeking to sustain a movement must protect his or her supporters.

Blacks stopped marching. The prevailing logic was: If injured in a demonstration on Sunday, they might not be able to work on Monday; which would mean a short paycheck on Friday; and that translated into the inability to make that luxury car payment on Tuesday.

CHAPTER 27

AFRICAN AMERICAN ASSIMILATION

During the Vietnam War, fighting age African Americans enrolled in College to take advantage of the Educational deferment typically reserved for the rich children of other ethnic persuasions. The number of African Americans enrolled in college more than doubled from 360,000 in 1967 to 727,000 in 1972. Sixteen percent of African Americans between the ages of 18 and 24 were enrolled in college compared with twenty five percent of whites.

During the sixties and seventies college educated African Americans slowly assimilated into the mainstream work force. They were afforded limited managerial positions in government, the military, and Social Service agencies. The number of African American professionals also increased significantly during this time period.

Although the income gap between Whites and African Americans remained substantial, it closed slightly. But, by the end of 1969 the steady rate of African American progress had been arrested. There was no relief in sight.

-1-

RECESSION SET-BACK

In the year 1970, the U.S. median family income was $9,870. America was spending billions on the war in Vietnam. The dollar was weak as we slipped into the throes of Stagflation – *"stagnant economic growth at a time when prices are rising."*

America was beset by double-digit interest rates and a 14% inflation rate. Although the price of crude oil was holding steady at $3.00 per barrel, gas at the full serve pump was a whopping .34 cents per gallon.

That year, America underwent one of its worst recessions – *"two consecutive quarters of negative GDP growth."* Unlike the Japanese who pioneered communications technology, Post World War II, America had specialized in the manufacture of aircraft. Due to lack of demand, firms in the aerospace industry were forced to layoff workers by the tens of thousands. That caused a ripple affect throughout the entire jobs market. There were few if any jobs available.

Although all Americans were hit hard by this economic downturn, it was especially hard on African Americans, who had only recently begun to emerge from the cruelties of Jim Crow domination and its adjunct poverty.

The African-American population totaled 23 million in 1970. That accounted for about 11% of the total U.S. population. 3.5 million of those African Americans had migrated from the Agricultural South to the Industrial North. Many had recently been hired to work in factories.

As the economy slowed, so did consumer demand. Manufacturers were forced to cutback on production and its number of employees. The unwritten rule was "African Americans were the last to be hired and the first to be fired."

The 1970 recession impacted African Americans disproportionately. While the national unemployment rate was nearly 5%, the White unemployment rate was less than 4%; and the African American unemployment rate was 7%. Additionally, African Americans were also disproportionately represented among the 600,000-800,000 discouraged workers and

340,000 incarcerated Americans. Neither group was included in the base unemployment statistics.

-2-

AFRICAN AMERICAN PROGRESS

Following the 1970 recession, the restoration of industrial and production jobs helped to stabilize the United States economy. America's economic situation began to rebound. In 1971 the median U.S. family income finally exceeded $10,000. Specifically, it was $10,290.

That year thirty-seven percent of African American males were employed in middle-class occupations. They were doctors, lawyers, accountants and managers. Thirty percent of all African American workers earned $10,000 or more, and 12% earned $15,000 or more.

The African American population had begun to mature politically. Between 1964 and 1972, the number of African Americans of voting age increased from 10 million to 13 million. African Americans had begun to elect representatives who were willing to promote their interests. In 1972, there were 2,265 African American elected officials nationwide. By 1999 that number had risen to 8,940.

-3-

INTEGRATION AND BLACK BUSINESS DISPLACEMENT

The force of racial desegregation had begun to take root in most places in America. Absent that extraordinary racial barrier, African Americans began to assimilate into mainstream society. They were able to move about, pretty much as they pleased, and enjoy the trappings of society. Still they had to exercise common sense. An African American couldn't walk into a honky-tonk bar in Chicago's Bridgeport neighborhood or Jackson, Mississippi and expect to be well received.

This generation of middle-class African Americans moved their immediate families from the inner cities to the suburbs. They left other impoverished family members to fend for themselves. Absent these learned individuals, African American neighborhoods were devoid of the skill and leadership necessary to develop and maintain family-owned businesses. Ambitious migrant merchants rushed to fill the void.

Heretofore, African Americans who were fortunate enough to vacation traveled by train, bus or car, to visit relatives in the South. Yet, the emerging African American bourgeoisie joined the "jet set." They boarded flying machines and traveled to Europe and the Caribbean.

118

Upon their return home from trips abroad, they showed off the latest designer fashions, not available at the local retail shop and boasted of the finer foods, not sold in the corner grocery store. Other African Americans, bitten by the curiosity bug, eagerly explored the shops and emporiums where Whites spent their money.

-4-

SHOPPING WHILE BLACK

Because there was no reciprocity, Integration was detrimental to the African American community. African Americans shopped at A&P, Wieboldt's Saks Fifth Avenue, and Macy's. But Whites did not shop at Chatham Food Store in Chicago. African American-owned stores sold Wonder bread and Campbell's soup, but White owned stores did not sell Baldwin ice cream or Parker House sausages. The influx of African American dollars increased the coffers of White owned businesses. But African American businesses suffered as their previously loyal customer base investigated this different culture.

The more astute African Americans recognized the danger inherent in a one-sided economic arrangement and warned against it. But crossovers shoppers countered with trumped-up complaints that African American shop owners were unsophisticated and their clerks treated them poorly. Those who naively perpetuated this

119

argument, which flew in the face of reason, frustrated the critics of Integration.

Those same African Americans continued to shop in White owned stores even though white clerks looked right through them with disdain and went out of their way to avoid assisting them. African Americans were regularly ignored and left standing at checkout counters for long periods of time. Seemingly, they were only visible to the suspicious security guards who followed them throughout the store. Someone wiser than myself termed this experience "Shopping While Black."

-5-

BLACK ECONOMIC INSTABILITY

Between 1972 and 1979, coinciding with the advent of Integration, African Americans cut back on spending within their own communities. Many African American businesses began to falter. Auto Mechanic shops, Restaurants, Hotels, Motels, Bus and Cab Companies, Auto Dealers, and others in labor-intensive industries struggled to survive. Dr. Webb Evans of the United American Progress Association, and others, encouraged African Americans to "buy black."

The African American to White average income ratio went on a roller coaster ride. In 1964, the median income of African American families was 54% that of whites; in 1972 that figure rose to

59%. In 1974, the median income of African Americans was 63 percent that of Whites. However, in 2004, the income of a typical African American family plummeted to only 58 percent of the income of a typical white family's.

-6-

BLACK CONVENTION

The Congressional Black Caucus was established in 1969 with a total of 13 members. In 1972 they convened a National Black Political Convention in Gary, Indiana, and attracted 6,000 delegates. They met March 9th thru March 12th and developed comprehensive strategies and policies to address issues central to African Americans. The Black Agenda items included Economic Development, Capital Punishment, Education, Health Care, Employment, Housing, Income and Poverty.

Access, Influence and Capital are atoms in the same element. Delegates to the Gary Convention realized that if African Americans achieved access to the social, economic, and political institutions, they would have increased influence; and thereby improve their access to capital.

That Convention is credited with enabling African Americans to inventory their assets, focus their efforts and thereby increase their political power and economic impact.

121

Government has gotten away from its core mission. The size of government has more to do with patronage than any need fulfillment. Patronage drives pork barrel spending and allows politicians to reward their friends and punish their enemies.

CHAPTER 28

GOVERNMENTAL DIVIDE

Government has grown so big that "We the People" have been besieged by bureaucracy. There are separate governmental bodies and agencies to address every concern imaginable. Although we're taxed to finance the operations of those agencies, we're stonewalled whenever we try to access the services they're mandated to provide.

Government's turn to technology has not made it any easier for our senior citizens and others trapped beyond the Digital Divide. Any information pertaining to government services is available via the Internet. However, that information is not reasonably accessible to people who don't have a computer with a broadband connection.

Even a simple phone call to City Hall can be a frustrating experience. An automated system answers and recites a menu of prompts. Seems it never includes the prompt that will patch you through to the person you need to speak with. Heaven help hard-of-hearing Grandma, who still uses the rotary phone.

The world in which we live has grown complex. That complexity is mainly due to the ever-expanding role of government in our lives. The government directs our every action from the time we awake until we go to sleep. It is hard to imagine the simple life before sophisticated communities. Once upon a time, Man was king of his cave. But that was then and this is now.

-1-

PRIVATIZATION

With the proliferation of Privatization, the lines between Governmental bodies and private entities have become blurred. Some people think Federal Express is a government agency. *A Federal Express agent knocked on a man's door. The man asked, "Who is it?" "Federal Express" the agent replied. The man nervously asked, "You got a search warrant?"* My point is it's easier to hold people accountable when you know what their responsibilities are.

The concept of Privatization - *outsourcing of labor intensive governmental services to a private contractor* - was first used by governmental bodies as a means of avoiding Labor Union requirements that resulted in excessive costs. For example, unions operating in Chicago required three employees on each city garbage truck, although most studies confirmed only two were necessary.

Unscrupulous politicians now use privatization as a means of continuing the Patronage systems that fuel their political machines. Patronage is *the hiring, firing or awarding of government contracts to political supporters.* It is illegal to use government resources to reward political workers or financial contributors. However, an entity that is awarded contracts to provide a government service is not similarly restricted. That private entity may hire and fire personnel and award sub-contracts at will.

Blackwater is a private military company under contract with the U.S. State Department. That government sanctioned private contractor, active in Iraq, often engages in hostilities. Unlike the U.S. military, Blackwater's activities, including employment practices, escape Congressional scrutiny.

In addition, privatization allows political machines to sidestep scrutiny due to activity that could be considered discriminatory.

Discrimination is *"the unfair or unlawful treatment of a person or persons within a protected class because of their race, age, or gender."* A government contractor is subject to less scrutiny and able to hire supporters of a political machine to the exclusion of all others.

Privatization has also proven effective as a means of avoiding the requirements of affirmative action programs. Affirmative Action is *"a means of nullifying proven past discrimination by mandating the inclusion of diverse groups, promoting outreach, and allowing the consideration of race, age or gender as a means of achieving reasonable targets and goals."* The Affirmative Action requirements applicable to governmental bodies do not necessarily transfer to its contractors.

Wherever there is an effort to correct the effects of discrimination, there is the potential for reverse discrimination – *harm to innocents as a consequence of dispensation ordered to cure the injustice that injured a select group of people.* The line that separates the two is thin. Therefore, it must be walked with due diligence and sensitivity.

In the last 25 years, union workers have declined from 20 percent to 12 percent of the U.S. labor force. These days, not much of anything is made within our shores. We have to make "made in America" mean something again.

CHAPTER 29

LABOR IMMIGRATION

*T*hroughout American history, its landowners and rich developers have relied upon immigrant workers. Some have been utilized to build the infrastructure of this vast and expansive nation; while others have been used to till the land and cultivate the crops.

Corporate America's preference has always been free labor. However, when that was not possible, cheap labor was a fine alternative. Cheap labor is assured when you have too many people seeking too few jobs.

Currently, Mexican Immigration is one of the most complex immigration issues in the realm of Globalization. Big Corporate interests who want fairly free labor have the most to gain from illegal Mexican immigration. Those corporations are proficient in their exploitation of undocumented

126

Mexicans, who desperately want to work. However, this is just the latest episode in the same old corporate playbook.

-1-

ORIGINAL MEXICAN IMMIGRATION

Although Mexico declared it independence from Spain on September 15, 1810, Mexican independence was not won until August 24, 1821. At that time Mexico was sparsely populated north of the Rio Grande by "mestizos," people of mixed European and North American Indigenous bloodlines.

The United States defeated Mexico in the 1848 battle for the right to annex Texas. There were 13,500 American casualties and 25,000 Mexican casualties. Following the Mexican-American War the United States purchased from Mexico much of the land that now constitutes our Southwestern border states.

The matter was formally resolved in the form of the Treaty of Guadalupe Hidalgo, signed February 2, 1848. The U.S. paid Mexico $15 million dollars, in exchange for California and Texas, and parts of Arizona, Colorado, Nevada, New Mexico, and Utah. Six years later, in the Gadsden Purchase, Mexico sold Arizona and the balance of New Mexico to their northern neighbor for $10 million dollars.

By treaty, the Mexican people that inhabited those lands were made citizens of the United States. However, they were eventually stripped of their ownership rights and chased across the border.

Because the U.S. government failed to protect them, and because they fled under duress, their descendents may have a valid Human Rights claim to citizenship.

When America's "Gentlemen's Agreement" with Japan banned Japanese immigration in 1907, cheap Mexican labor became a desired premium. But, hostile welcoming parties of bandits' cowboys and Texas Rangers greeted Mexican laborers who crossed the border. Motivated by the prospect of jobs in the United States and the Revolution in Mexico, immigrants came anyway. The 1930 U.S Census counted 600,000 Mexican immigrants. However, it is estimated that at least a million had crossed the border into El Paso, Texas, the southwestern Ellis Island.

-2-

MEXICAN REPATRIATION

The 1929 Stock Market crash, instigated the Great Depression that ravaged the economic stability of the United States and the entire industrial world. This severe economic slump lasted 10 years. Bank Foreclosures of homes and farms destabilized the Real Estate market. A tsunami of unemployment swept across America. Panic, hopelessness and despair were evident on the faces of hobos as they stood in the soup lines.

Mexican immigrant workers became expendable. Several hundred thousand migrant farm workers were repatriated to Mexico along with many United States citizens, of Mexican descent, who could not prove their citizenship. Those wrongful deportations might further bolster a Human Rights claim for U.S. citizenship.

-3-

BRACERO ACCORD

Mexican immigration took a new twist during World War II. To ensure the continued production of America's food supply, the United States and Mexico entered into the Bracero Accord. This agreement arranged for the importation of temporary Mexican agriculture workers.

Treatment of Mexican workers ranged from sub-standard to cruel. Many realized little or no actual pay from those employers who took mandatory deductions for food, clothing, shelter, and medical treatment. Throughout the Korean

War this program was beneficial to the Farm Grower's associations who supported it. Their members skirted the rules to take full advantage of the opportunity for increased profits.

By 1954 Illegal immigration had become part and parcel of the American economy. Even the Immigration and Naturalization Service, which launched an initiative called "Operation Wetback" that apprehended one million illegal immigrants, was careful not to have any real effect. With a wink and a nod, INS officials quickly reprocessed those undocumented braceros and returned them to the field. This program rife with conflict officially ended in 1964 when President Kennedy heeded to pressure from the farm worker's unions.

-4-

IMMIGRATION REFORM

The Hart-Celler Immigration Reform Act of 1965 staged the elimination of immigration quotas, imposed by the 1924 Immigration Act. As a result, the number of Mexican migrant farm workers increased dramatically.

On November 6, 1986 President Ronald Reagan signed the Immigration Reform Control Act, which made it illegal for anyone to hire an undocumented worker; required employers to confirm a potential employee's immigration status; and granted amnesty to those undocumented immigrants who, for at least four years, had continuously lived in the United States.

Much to the chagrin of the Mexican government, this Act was conceived unilaterally.

-5-

CESAR CHAVEZ

Cesar Chavez was born on March 31, 1927, in Yuma, Arizona. Recognized as a great American Civil Rights leader, he co-founded the United Farm Workers Association in 1962. This organization, initially formed to help workers secure their unemployment benefits, quickly became one that fought for the rights, wages and safe working conditions of Latino migrant farm workers.

Cesar Chavez was active mostly in California and the Southwest throughout the 1970s. He successfully spearheaded worker strikes and boycotts of lettuce and grapes grown with poisonous pesticides. In 1975, fifteen million Americans supported his worldwide grape boycott. Chavez became famous for his personal sacrifice and hunger strikes.

Chavez opposed the Mexico-United States' policies of legal and illegal immigration as a means of keeping wages low. He understood the loss of bargaining power and negative job market effects inherent in the practice of flooding the country with unskilled workers. A survey by the Pew Hispanic Center conducted in 2002 found, "48 percent of registered Latino voters felt that there were too many immigrants in the U.S. while only 7 percent thought there were too few."

Chavez, who died on April 23, 1993, is celebrated as a modern American hero with numerous public facilities named in his honor.

-6-

CHINESE EXCLUSION ACT

Today's Chinese population migrated to the United States in three major waves. The initial wave began in 1849 at a time when the surface gold in California was plentiful. These men and women from the Far East were called "Orientals." When gold became rare, the Chinese prospectors were attacked and threatened and eventually forced from their mines.

The second wave came during the 1860s as Chinese laborers. They joined the labor gangs and helped to build this nation's Railroads. They were paid very little for their services.

At the end of the Civil War, members of the Workingman's Party blamed the Chinese immigrant workers for the unfavorable jobs market. An anti-Chinese sentiment began to sweep across America. That strong sentiment was often expressed in the form of the racial slur "coolies."

In 1880, America revised the Burlingame Treaty of 1868 and established the power to suspend immigration. Congress quickly acted to suspend Chinese immigration. They then passed the Chinese Exclusion Act on May 6, 1882.

This Act excluded Chinese from U.S. citizenship. The Magnuson Act passed in 1943 repealed the Chinese Exclusion Act and imposed a quota of 150 Chinese immigrants per year. That was the law of the land until Congress passed the 1965 Immigration Act.

Today many American Corporations are outsourcing jobs in the professional, technology, and customer service related fields. India is the most prominent beneficiary of that emerging policy. This has proved harmful to American jobs market. The character of the American workforce has gone from one of industrial manufacturer to Service workers.

This policy is also devastating to the domestic Economy. The most egregious American corporations incorporate offshore to avoid paying taxes, receive U.S. Government contracts, and outsource the work to foreign workers. This represents a lose - lose scenario for America.

"So, first of all, let me assert my firm belief that the only thing we have to fear is fear itself - nameless, unreasoning, unjustified terror, which paralyzes needed efforts to convert retreat into advance."

Franklin Delano Roosevelt

CHAPTER 30

LEGACY OF FREEDOM

A record number of Americans are having a record number of babies. With one person born alive every 8 seconds, there are at least 10,500 people born in the United States every single day. However, as morbid as it may seem, we are all born to die.

Death is as much a part of life as life itself. Each day approximately 6,800 Americans die. Yet, life goes on. We bury our dead with dignity and keep on living.

Life on Earth is a constant fight with death. No one emerges from that fight alive. Some people fight and die young. Others fight and live to be a hundred years of age, or more. In the end; it matters not how long you fought to live; it matters only that you fought to live free.

It is imperative that our generation honors the traditions pioneered by our forbearers. Those Americans never cowered in a corner in fear of being slaughtered. They marched headlong into the tempest, committed to the preservation of the freedoms that have enabled succeeding generations to breathe free. They left us a legacy of liberty.

During bitter periods of adversity fearless soldiers patrolled remote outposts to protect the liberties that have been handed down from generation to generation. They gallantly persevered even in the face of threats seen and unseen. They hoped and prayed that our commitment to freedom would remain as relentless as the waves that forever pound our shores.

The unyielding will to persist punctuates the American legacy of courage. But, there are times when courage is not enough.

Safety matters, but our freedoms and our inalienable rights are indispensable and non-negotiable. These fixtures, vital to the framework of the Constitution, are not ours to give away.

CHAPTER 31

AMERICA'S FREEDOM COMPROMISED

On the morning of September 11, 2001, in a series of four related attacks, nineteen Al-Qaeda terrorists killed three thousand innocent people. They hijacked four commercial airliners and crashed one into each of the World Trade Center towers, one into the Pentagon, and one into a Pennsylvania field. Fifteen of the hijackers were from Saudi Arabia and none were from Iraq.

An unhealthy paranoia swept across America. Fearful Americans encouraged Racial Profiling - *"the invidious reliance upon race or ethnic characteristics to determine the likelihood that a person will engage in criminal behavior."* At first, they only gave law enforcement officials a limited license to accost anyone who appeared to be of Middle Eastern decent. However, intense fear led Americans to quickly allow the Security procedures based upon Racial Profiling to escalate into a complete security blanket.

136

Everyone was treated like a suspect. It didn't matter whether a person fit some "profile" or not. Although this violated the Equal Protection Clause of the Fourteenth Amendment, even Civil libertarians didn't fight the fear driven power.

The "USA PATRIOT" Act, an acronym for, *Uniting and Strengthening America by Providing Appropriate Tools Required to Intercept and Obstruct Terrorism,* was passed on October 26, 2001. Among other things, it authorized law enforcement officials to eavesdrop on phone calls, intercept emails, examine people's financial and medical records, and enter private residences or businesses to sneak and peek, all without specific court approval.

To qualify to board an airplane or enter some government buildings, law abiding American citizens now must submit to an intrusive search of person and belongings. Grandma, whose specialty is baked Apple Pie, can't even hop aboard an Amtrak train without a government I.D. card.

Fifteen years ago, if someone had forecast the implementation of these extreme security procedures we would have thought they were bonkers. We would have retorted, "Not in America; not in a million years." Our acceptance of these procedures emphasizes our lack of regard for freedom.

We cannot allow the threat of terrorism to force us to abdicate our ideals. Ironically, our noble soldiers, who voluntarily serve in Iraq and Afghanistan, are willing to die to preserve our right to live free. Yet, those of us who remain at home are willing to compromise our civil liberties to preserve our individual safety.

This "land of the free and home of the brave" should saddle-up and protect its citizens and secure its porous borders through vigilant democratic means.

-1-

HOMELAND SECURITY

The Department of Homeland Security was created to provide greater protection on the heels of the tragic terrorist events. That department was initially under the direction of Tom Ridge, who had served two-terms as governor of Pennsylvania. Secretary Ridge resigned on December 1, 2004 and on February 15, 2005 was replaced by former Judge Michael Chertoff.

When the Federal Emergency Management Agency, headed by Michael D. Brown, was placed under the Department of Homeland Security in 2003, FEMA's focus shifted from Emergency catastrophe management to mostly terrorism related pursuits.

On November 19, 2001 President Bush signed the Aviation and Transportation Security Act. Under that authority, the Transportation Security Administration agency of Department of Transportation was empowered to regulate security within the nation's airports. TSA's stringent security measures have resulted in long lines and the overall inconvenience of travelers. However people were willing to tolerate all of this because the President said it would make us safer. In fact, safety was only an illusion.

The Seattle Times documented a hundred instances of security breaches that have been reported since TSA screeners assumed responsibility for airport security. These include instances where people were allowed to board planes with knives or carpenter's tools, including a hammer and other items that could be considered weapons. The Times article alleged, "Screeners say that's a fraction of the incidents, and most are never disclosed." Granted, it may unreasonable to expect any security system to be 100% efficient; However, people who have willingly given up their freedoms deserve more than a mere illusion of safety.

-2-

LIQUIDS IN BAGGIES FARCE

On August 10, 2006 British authorities reportedly foiled a plot to use liquid explosives to destroy airplanes. In response, the next day TSA banned all liquids and gels from carry-on bags. Caught off-guard, Air-travelers were forced to throw away expensive medications, baby formulas, toiletries and perfumes.

On September 26, 2006 TSA eased its liquid restrictions. Thereafter, passengers allowed to carryon 3-ounce containers of liquids, as long as they were in clear plastic Baggies. If a traveler arrived at the TSA security checkpoint without those permissible carryons being in a Baggie, they were discarded. That is unless the traveler was willing to take the items to the car and, once again, stand in the 2 to 3 hour long security lines.

TSA officials acted as if Baggies magically rendered harmless any potentially explosive liquids contained therein. Keep in mind; once passengers cleared the TSA security checkpoint they were free to remove the liquid containers from their Baggie at anytime.

This entire security procedure was illogical. For, if several co-conspirators each carried 3-ounces of explosive through the security checkpoint, there was nothing to prevent them from combining their portions, once inside the terminal Furthermore, all would have access to their Baggies and the liquids contained therein, at various points and time during the flight. Thus, the procedure served no legitimate purpose.

According to the FBI those liquids posed no real threat. That fact was acknowledged by the heads of the TSA and the American Chemical Society, in a USA Today story, posted on September 26, 2006. The USA Today article informed,

"Passengers will be allowed to carry liquids on airplanes under new security rules prompted by FBI tests that show it's highly unlikely that terrorists could bring down a jet with a bomb made from small amounts of fluids, the nation's airport security chief said Monday. Travelers may bring liquids and everyday items such as shampoo, toothpaste and makeup through security, provided they're stored in 3-ounce containers that fit in a 1-quart clear bag, Transportation Security Administration chief Kip Hawley said Monday. Passengers also can carry on liquids and gels in any quantity that they buy in airport shops after passing through security, including at duty-free shops. Drinks and other items are screened before being sold in secure airport areas. Testing by the FBI and at government labs showed that small containers of liquids "don't pose a real threat,' Hawley said.' Jim Kapin, head of health and safety for the American Chemical Society, said small quantities of liquids could not seriously damage an airplane. Even if several terrorists smuggled liquid explosives on board, it is 'practically speaking, impossible' to make a bomb on an airplane because of the equipment and expertise required, Kapin said."

-3-

REAL I.D.

Alarmingly, President Bush signed the Real ID Act into law on May 11, 2005. When that Act goes into effect Americans seeking to open bank accounts, enter federal buildings or get on planes, will be required to present I.D. that meets prescribed security and authentication criterion.

Several State legislatures are opposed to the Real ID system. Under this law all states will be required to transfer their Department of Motor Vehicle records into a national database. In a letter addressed to Colorado Governor Bill Ritter dated January 18, 2008, Montana Governor Brian Schweitzer cautioned,

> "Last year the Montana Legislature unanimously passed, and I signed, a bill to prevent our state from participating in the Real ID [Mont. Code. Ann. Sec 61-5-128 (2007)]. We recognized that Real ID was a major threat to the privacy, constitutional rights, and pocketbooks of ordinary Montanans. We now have a strong law on the books barring implementation in our state."

I received my Illinois Driver's License in 1972. It was a simple colorful card with my name,

142

address, date of birth, height, weight, hair color, eye color and my driver's license number, imprinted on it. It had no picture, hologram or bar code. There was no such thing as a State I.D. card. Back then the only time you needed any I.D. was if you wanted to purchase liquor or drive a car. If you were walking down the street and the police had probable cause to stop you, they simply asked your name. There was no computer in the car, to enable them to run an instant background check. Now police officers stop you without cause. The first thing they ask is to see your I.D. If you have none you are presumed to be a vagrant, and are subject to arrest.

I am reminded of the shock I experienced the first time I heard that South Afrikaners routinely required South African's blacks and Coloureds to carry their "Apartheid papers." First adopted in 1809 and regularly amended thereafter, the "Pass Laws" rigidly controlled the movement of black laborers between rural and urban areas. Each year hundreds of thousands were jailed for not having those papers. The more blacks resisted the Pass Laws, the more rigid the requirements became.

By 1948 there were South African Pass Laws in 265 "proclaimed" urban areas. In 1952 The Natives Act consolidated the eleven Pass Laws of the various areas into one universal Reference Book, which fully documented every black man or woman's personal information and work history. It was illegal for them to be without their book. I am appalled to see America now implementing Pass Laws, in the form of a National I.D. card.

-4-

WAR AGAINST TERRORISM

In response to the worst terrorist attack on U.S. soil, President Bush, a clout heavy Texas Oilman by profession, promised to bring Al-Qaeda leader Osama Bin Laden to justice. However, he never demonstrated the will or committed the resources necessary to capture that son of a Saudi Arabian. His ties to the bin Ladens were too deep.

The Bush administration declared war on terrorism. They penalized nations suspected of harboring terrorist groups operating within their borders. Joined by the United Kingdom, the U.S. initiated a war against terrorist in Afghanistan.

Then in 2003, under the pretext that Iraq had weapons of mass destruction; the Bush administration preemptively invaded that oil-rich country. He completely ignored the principle that War is supposed to be the engagement of last resort. Bush relentlessly bombarded the people of Iraq, during a tremendous aerial assault, which he affectionately called "Shock and Awe."

Once on the ground, Coalition forces secured the Oil fields but exposed Iraq's cultural artifacts to looting. Americans found no weapons of mass destruction; no connection to Al Qaeda; imprisoned President Saddam Hussein and witnessed his execution.

-5-

PRICE OF WAR

As of March 1, 2008, a total of 3,973 U.S. Military personnel, 174 U.K. soldiers, and 133 other Coalition Forces have lost their lives, in the Iraqi war. More than one hundred-thousand Iraqui civillians have also been killed. Because of the war, America is distracted and unable to focus on the domestic needs of its people. The U.S. deficit is approaching $410 billion dollars. The nation is teetering on the brink of a recession. Risky lending schemes have resulted in a nationwide mortgage foreclosure crisis, which is threatening the home ownership of millions of Americans. At the same time, major banks are folding.

In February of 2008 our national debt was $9 trillion dollars. It rises daily as America borrows hundreds of billions of dollars from China and India. The Bush administration is spending $11 billion dollars a month on the wars in Iraq and Afghanistan. At the same time, Bush refuses to repeal the tax breaks given to the rich. Common sense says you cannot increase your spending, at a time when your income is reduced. Yet, Bush persists unabashed and unashamed, in the

145

promotion of a war and unsound economic policies that have resulted in increased oil prices, which enrich his former investment partners.

With $17,000, Bush founded Arbusto Oil Company in 1977. Among his investors was terrorist Osama bin Laden's brother Salem bin Laden of the Saudi Binladin Group. After Salem died in a 1988 plane crash, his Arbusto interest passed to NCB bank owner Khalid bin Mahfouz, who immediately contributed $270,000 dollars to Osama bin Laden's terrorist organization.

In 1982, one year after his father was elected U.S. Vice President; George W. changed the company name from Arbusto Oil, to Bush Exploration. Numerous investors contributed excessively large sums of money in exchange for small percentages of ownership. For example, when Arbusto was worth only $400,000, Phillip Uzielli invested $1 million dollars for a 10% ownership share.

Bush Exploration and Spectrum 7 Energy Corp merged in 1984. Bush became Chairman and CEO. Two years later, Harken Energy purchased that failing company. Bush joined its Board of Directors. In 1990, one week before Harken went bust, Bush sold his stock for $845,560. The SEC investigated him for insider trading. Yet, because the makeup of that regulatory board politically favored the Bush family, the memo stating it had found no infraction remains suspect.

Big money buys big government influence. The people in corporate suits groom the candidates and finance their campaigns, in exchange for huge tax breaks and contracts at the expense of working class stiffs.

CHAPTER 32

MISJUSTICE

*J*ames Madison, who helped to frame the United States Constitution and campaigned for its ratification, warned against the dominating potential of "factions." Those groups Madison called factions, are what we now call "Special Interest." Special Interest groups are *the wealthy organizations and their lobbyist who are able to influence governmental outcomes that may be adverse to the interest of average citizens.*

They are the land barons, energy companies, oil tycoons, growers, manufacturers, bomb makers, and media moguls. They dictate our local, national and international agendas. The profit motives of special interest groups drive America's policies relating to energy, war, incarceration, education, poverty, insurance and healthcare, just to name a few.

Madison warned that the factions might dominate government and override the people's will. To wit, Special Interest groups have financed winning campaigns and thereby, purchased the loyalty of our representatives. The people elect politicians to serve in their best interest, and the lobbyists get the key to their office back door. This consolidation of big money interest and big power players is the incarnation of the unholy quid-pro-quo alliance Madison warned against.

America's population has now topped 300 million. There are more people in this nation than ever before. However the will of the people is no match for the power wielded by the consolidated Mega Corporations and Political Machines.

"We the working class stiffs," Native Americans, African Americans, Latinos, Whites, and Asians; Middle Class and Impoverished, have become a hopeless people. Many of us are convinced that no matter what we do we cannot effectively compete against those consolidated empires.

Because of campaign contributions from Special Interests, the coffers of members of the U. S. House of Representatives and U.S. Senate "runneth over." It is extremely difficult for the average person to mount a winning campaign against them. To minimize the effect of these alliances, we must impose term limits. Similar to the U.S. President, no Congressman or Senator should be allowed to serve more than two-four year terms, within any particular legislative branch. That period of time would be sufficient for any able legislator to develop the relationships needed to champion major pieces of legislation. Thereafter, they can run for some other National, State, County or Local municipal office.

-1-

ELECTORAL DISENFRANCHISEMENT

A growing percentage of people are unwilling or unable to participate in the Electoral process. In 1960, 63.1% of the voting age population participated in that Presidential election, whereas only 55.3% of the voting age population participated in the 2004 Presidential election.

Florida, and other states have permanently revoked every ex-felon's right to vote, irrespective of the nature of their crime. In certain states, thirteen percent of African American men are ineligible to vote.

The waning level of participation in the Electoral Process is a warning sign that an alarming number of citizens are being disenfranchised. Many African American Floridians who were registered to vote in the 2000 Presidential elections were denied the right to vote. Law-abiding citizens were racially profiled and intimidated by police.

While in the vicinity of their designated polling places they were detained and unreasonably asked whether they were ex-felons or under correctional supervision. Meanwhile, inside the polling places, people's registration was unfairly being challenged.

Palm Beach, Florida voters complained of ballot irregularities and ballot tampering. Statistical data supported voter allegations that the "butterfly" ballot, with two pages that open up like wings, was confusing and that arrows from the candidate's names to the punch holes were misleading. As opposed to the one-half of one percent nationwide norm, a full four percent punched for both Democrat Party Candidate Al Gore and Reform Party Candidate Pat Buchanan. In total, 19,000 double-punched Palm Beach ballots were invalidated.

Polling place judges refused to assist confused voters and refused to replace spoiled ballots upon request, as required by law. The votes of many other Floridian's simply did not count because the chads were hanging or insufficiently dimpled.

-2-

BUSH V. GORE

Democrat Al Gore won the popular vote, 51,003,926 votes to Republican George W.

Bush's 50,460,110 votes. However, the election would be decided by the results in Florida.

After several Florida State court battles, a partial vote recount and an unusual United States Supreme Court decision that prematurely stopped the vote recount, George Bush was declared the winner in Florida by a mere 537 vote margin. Once awarded Florida's 25 Electoral College votes, he had a total of 271 compared to Al Gore's 266 Electoral College votes. Thus, Bush became President of the United States, contrary to the will of the majority of voters.

The lesson learned is that the party that controls the voting apparatus and the electoral board or commission will always determine the winner.

Many of the voters who were frustrated by the outcome of the November 2000 Presidential election vowed never to vote again. But that response is illogical. It makes no sense to stop voting simply because things didn't go your way in a particular election. Paul Bunyon never knocked a tree down with the first swing of the axe.

Disappointed citizens must never give up on the voting process because of an undesirable election outcome. Instead, they should use the voting process to unseat undesirable politicians. When good people give up, bad politicians win.

-3-

INMATES SHOULD VOTE

Two states, Maine and Vermont, allow all inmates to vote in every election. Some states allow ex-felons to vote upon approval of their petition to the state. Unfortunately, many others permanently suspend their right to vote.

The rules vary from state-to-state because the right to vote is granted by state governments, not the federal government. However, if the Preamble to the Constitution has meaning, once people pay their debt to society, all rights must be restored.

Maine and Vermont should not be the exception, but the rule. Nearly 5 million potential voters are denied the Right to vote because of their ex-felon status. Considering, the current rate of incarceration and current state policies, the percentage of African American men denied the right to vote could eclipse 40 per cent. To avert the potential of this continuing injustice, Human Rights activists must develop a plan to fight state-by-state to ensure everyone's Voting Rights.

-4-

THE BIG UNEASY

Hurricane Katrina is not legendary because of her rating as a Category 4 storm. Both hurricanes

Charley and Dennis achieved that same rating based upon the Saffir-Simpson Scale. Nor is Katrina infamous because of her death toll in the thousands. The Galveston, Texas Hurricane of 1900 holds the record with 8,000 killed.

Katrina is a most notable event due to the United States Federal Emergency Management Agency's failure to respond once the levees broke. The lack of decisive action on the part of FEMA officials was at least incompetent. Because the chain of events that occurred in the immediate aftermath of the storm was anticipated, the inaction of those officials was borderline criminal.

FEMA completed a $1 million dollar Category 3 hurricane simulation in 2004. It concluded that the water would overflow the levees and floods would devastate Southeast Louisiana. The United States took no action to avoid this potential danger.

In 2005, the New Orleans, Louisiana metropolitan area was one of the poorest in the nation. It had one of the lowest median income ratings and one of the highest poverty rates. Twenty eight percent of its households were without private transportation. A half-million New Orleans residents were living below sea level surrounded by Lake Pontchartrain and the Mississippi River.

By the time Katrina ravaged the Gulf Coast on August 29, 2005, with wind speed in excess of 131 miles per hour, hundreds of thousands had been evacuated from New Orleans. But tens of thousands poor, transportation challenged, elderly, ill, disabled, mostly African American residents had been left behind.

The institutional racial overtones were evident from the start. The survivors who rushed to the New Orleans Superdome to escape the rapidly rising floodwaters were quickly labeled "refugees," and thus effectively dehumanized. Officials described African American survivors seen entering flood-damaged stores in search of food and clothing as "looters." Whites seen doing the same thing were said to be "finding supplies."

-5-

THE SUPERDOME

Fifteen thousand survivors made their way to the New Orleans Superdome, which had previously been designated a safe spot. The city had stockpiled limited amounts of food and water therein. Those supplies were quickly exhausted and conditions immediately became life threatening. Despite having loads of food and water on trucks staged in the vicinity, FEMA provided no relief.

Members of the media were able to move in and out of the Superdome without putting their lives at risk. Television news crews reported unfounded rumors of Superdome savagery and rape. Newscasters pleaded with the Government to act quickly to rescue those helpless human beings who were growing more and more desperate by the minute.

FEMA heard the pleas of those stranded residents. But they did not mount an effort to assist them. FEMA officials remained at a distance monitoring the deteriorating situation. Meanwhile, under the guise of Emergency relief, FEMA officials' were setting-up military bases in the region to control any dissidents. FEMA made no attempt to deliver needed supplies until September 2, 2005.

Largely due to FEMA's failure to act decisively, more than 5,000 people died. 1.4 million people were displaced, three-fourths of them permanently. Families were separated.

-6-

DOLPHINS, DOGS AND CATS

On September 15th there were volunteers still going from door to door looking for survivors. Human bodies were lying in the streets throughout the flood zone. The death toll was hovering around eleven hundred, and at least ten thousand people were missing and unaccounted for.

At that time, the collective news media turned its attention to the search for animals and sea mammals. The headlines and news teasers were dominated by the search for the 17 dolphins swept from the aquarium and the many dogs and cats displaced by the storm. Stories concerning the rescue of potential survivors or the recovery of human bodies were mysteriously wiped from the headlines, once and for all.

-7-

BUSH-FEMA FUMES

The United States House of Representatives Select Bipartisan Committee to Investigate the Preparation for and Response to Hurricane Katrina found former head of the Army Corps of Engineers James Witt oversaw the reports, which warned such a disaster could occur. There was no justification for the Bush administration's claim that they were caught off guard.

The Bush administration claimed they had no knowledge of water overflowing the levees until two days after the storm. The morning following the storm FEMA official Marty Bahamonde took a helicopter ride and confirmed massive flooding.

Bahamonde phoned his report into FEMA, which at 9:27 P.M. sent an official email report to Secretary Michael Chertoff as well as the chief of staff of the Department of Homeland Security. FEMA director Michael Brown personally notified the White House of the flooding by midnight.

Neither President Bush nor Michael Chertoff ordered any action be taken. It was as if they thought they could close their eyes and make the flooding go away. The Media did not become aware of the flooding until two days after Katrina had come and gone.

At the time Katrina hit, FEMA Director Michael D. Brown may have been under qualified and insensitive. According to professionals in the emergency management area, there was no other reasonable excuse for his lack of response. However, even if the director were all of those things, that wouldn't explain an entire agency's failure to act.

To the untrained eye, it appears as though someone higher up the food chain put the clamps on the New Orleans emergency response efforts. Some suspect Brown was merely the scapegoat for the Bush administration, whose motives remain suspect.

Two years after the storm, more than 1,000 people were still missing.

The loss of opportunity is more than a slap in the face; it's a kick down the stairs.

CHAPTER 33

INTERNATIONAL HUMAN RIGHTS

*H*istorically, traditions, customs, as well as language and cultural differences were insurmountable in the business sense. Those factors inhibited trade between divergent groups of people located in different regions of the world. We now operate in a Global Economy. Average individuals are afforded the opportunity to engage in trade and compete for business worldwide.

The modern Global Economy was made possible by the rigorous development of a global civil society – Non-Governmental Organizations such as churches and community groups. NGOs spearheaded the development of the capacity to communicate and cooperate across all linguistic, geographical, political, cultural, sociological, philosophical, ideological and religious barriers. The advent of the Internet is responsible for the formation of more productive working relations between all humanitarian groups that subscribe to the United Nations.

The U.N. International Charter is premised upon principles, which promote dignity and equality for all. On December 10, 1948 this body issued a "Universal Declaration of Human Rights." This proclamation serves as an International mean, which obligates every individual and institution to advocate respect for the rights and freedoms we all cherish.

The United Nations Committee on the Elimination of Racial Discrimination (CERD), which became effective on January 4, 1969, is the international body of independent experts that monitors implementation of the Convention. This Convention is the principal of agreement that mandates the bi-annual reporting of the initial participating nations and others that later accede to the Convention. The United States is signatory to the CERD.

The United States Justice Department is responsible for enforcing the law and defending America against threats foreign and domestic, and ensuring impartial justice for all Americans. That agency ensures our adherence to the Convention of the CERD. More specifically, in the International Human Rights arena, the Civil Rights Division of the Justice Department is supposed to make certain we are CERD compliant.

To date, the United States has not been forthright and honest with CERD panelists. Official U.S.

reports do not accurately reflect America's failure to address Institutional Racism. As suggested by CERD, America should empower an agency specifically charged with the responsibility to completely eliminate Racism.

-1-

HUMAN DECENCY

We must be relentless in our fight to eradicate the last vestiges of inequality and oppression in America. This is the modern moral imperative. If we fail, another generation will inherit the curse of Institutional Racism.

Therefore, Americans must wage a campaign for Human Rights and Human Decency as comprehensive as the historic campaigns for Civil Rights and Voting Rights.

It is our duty as human beings to address the modern human rights abuses affecting families throughout the United States of America. It is our duty to draw a roadmap that will lead this nation back to the intersection of Dignity and Self-respect.

-2-

DISPARATE IMPACT

We cannot continue to turn a blind eye to the modern day injustices that interfere with people's access to opportunity. We must act to eliminate the racial disparities in Education, Health, Prosecution, Voting, Hiring, and the like.

Title VII of the Civil Rights Act of 1964 (Title VII), prohibits discrimination in the workplace on the basis of race, color, religion, sex, or national origin. The Supreme Court has previously held, that disparate treatment claims under Title VII require proof of discriminatory intent. However, in Reeves v. Sanderson Plumbing Products, Inc., 120 S. Ct. 2097 (2000), the United States Supreme Court unanimously held an employee could prevail in a discrimination suit without proving intent or providing express evidence of discrimination.

A common characteristic of all disparate treatment cases is the lack of direct evidence of the intent to discriminate. Thus, under the current law, unless there is a smoking gun, the average plaintiff will not prevail.

We must campaign for the universal application of a standard that allows for the finding of a disparate impact or the finding of discrimination based upon proof that the practice more harshly impacts one group as opposed to all others, without an acceptable justification. Under this standard, intent would be irrelevant.

In other words if it looks like a duck, waddles like a duck, and quacks like a duck, Let's call it a duck. We don't have to wait for DNA test results. If people within a protected group are negatively impacted, no matter what the intent, it's discrimination.

-3-

PRISON INDUSTRIAL COMPLEX

The United States Penal institutions have become profit centers for big business and small town interests. There are legislators who will confess their desire to build jails transcends any interest in building schools. A town, which builds a prison, must also build access roads, sewer and septic systems, as well as lighting systems. They need hotels, restaurants and shops to accommodate visitors.

The Thirteenth amendment to the U.S. Constitution officially abolished slavery except for those persons convicted of a crime. That loophole allows America to lock citizens up and throw away the key. Absent that exception, persons convicted of a crime could challenge their incarceration on the basis of a fundamental denial of Human Rights.

According to Department of Justice Federal Bureau of Investigation statistics, reported on January 7, 2008, violent and non-violent crime is down in every category. Yet, the United States prison and jail population has swelled to 2.3 million inmates.

One out of every one hundred Americans is in prison or in jail. This is largely attributable to initiatives such as mandatory sentencing and the three strikes law. In 2003 the U.S. Supreme Court held in both Ewing v. California and Lockyer v. Andrade, that the three strikes law, also known as, habitual offender laws, did not constitute cruel or unusual punishment in violation of the eighth amendment. Prosecutors have the power to grant exceptions, but Judges must abide by mandatory sentencing guidelines.

Both in terms of raw numbers and percentages, America incarcerates more people than any other country. Even China, a far more populous nation, is a distant second.

-4-

PRISONS FOR PROFIT

Despite America's promise of life, liberty, and the pursuit of happiness; our prison population is burgeoning. Non-violent Habitual drug users, who were not a danger to society, are being given longer sentences, warehoused in penal institutions, and separated from their families for inordinate periods of time. Their lengthy incarceration does not make America safer; it only bolsters the Prison Industrial Complex.

The Prison Industrial Complex, encompasses prison builders, prison employees and the various entities that provide products, goods and services to the state agencies that are responsible for the care and incarceration of prison inmates. The Special Interests that drive this monstrosity, are dependant upon the burgeoning prison population. Consequently, it is projected that our prison population will continue to increase.

According to Kentucky Governor Steve Beshear, although that state's crime rate has increased by only three percent since the 1970s, the state's incarceration rate increased by a whopping 600 percent. They had only 2,840 state prisoners in 1970. That number jumped to 22,440 by February of 2008.

Kentucky's inmate population grew 12 percent in 2007 alone. Kentucky taxpayers spent $450 million dollars to feed, shelter and provide other services to inmates. Nationally, incarceration costs an average of $31 thousand dollars a year per inmate.

In 1976 the U.S. Supreme Court confirmed the constitutional right of inmates to have access to health care. According to the National

Conference of State Legislatures, prison health care costs, particularly for elderly inmates, contributed to the 10% rise in state prison spending in 2006, up from fiscal year 2005.

Many states are grappling with issues pretaining to prison funding. Some have turned to one of the three primary types of Prison Privatization. The first type is publicly managed with all basic services provided by contractors. The next are publicly owned facilities managed by private firms. Finally, the third type is completely owned and operated by a private firm paid a fee to incarcerate inmate.

-5-

PRISON PROFITEERING

Profiteering from prisons is not limited to the rich. Average people buy stock in companies that manage prisons simply by trading on Wall Street. For example, Cornell Companies founded in 1991 is publicly traded on the New York Stock Exchange as CRN.

Cornell reported 2007 Fourth Quarter earnings of $5.4 million dollars, up from $4.7 million dollars during the same period of 2006. CRN traded at 37 cents per share, on February 13, 2008, which exceeded financial expert estimates of 31 cents per share. Prison privatization is not only steady business it is exceedingly lucrative.

Some firms have begun to profit from prison labor. According to state law, persons convicted of a crime can be made to work for corporations and manufacturers, willing to pay the state a nominal wage for each hour of inmate service. With no requirement of a benefits package, this "Penal labor" has proved beneficial to many manufacturing corporations. Typically, the lion's share of inmate wages are taken by the state to defray the cost of prison operations.

In many jurisdictions prisoners "Pay to Stay." Inmates are charged a daily rate to defray the cost of their incarceration. For example, under Missouri law, the attorney general may seize the assets of inmates, upon court approval. Missouri collected $384 thousand dollars from inmates in the first five months of 2004, according to State's Attorney spokesman Scott Holste. These funds are used to offset the cost of housing, food and medical care received while in prison.

There is something fundamentaly wrong when influential corporations and people profit from the incarceration of millions of people who don't necessarily belong in prison. We must act to reverse this trend of allowing people and organizations to profit from prison products and services.

Not-for-profits and humanitarian organizations should replace for profit entities in the food chain of the Prison Industrial Complex.

How long will it be before they grow tired of feeding the habitual offenders, with three strikes, and put them on death row?

CHAPTER 34

DEATH PENALTY

I know people who go to church on Sunday and support the Death Penalty on Monday. They can direct you, by chapter and verse, to the Lord's commandment, "Thou Shall not Kill," or the Lord's admonishment "Vengeance is mine." However, blinded by their desire for revenge, they cannot see the hypocrisy of their ways.

The Death penalty is yet another example of man's inhumanity towards man. The most powerful thing the state can do to a person, is take their life. Personally, there is no person or structured institution in society that I would trust with such tremendous power.

Justice is not blind, fair or impartial. Although African Americans are only 13 percent of the nation's population, we are 54 percent of the prison population. Whites use and sell drugs at a higher percentage rate than African Americans. However, African Americans are ten times more likely to be incarcerated.

167

Amongst the drug abuser community, there is now a higher Black to White incarceration ratio. On average, African Americans are serving longer sentences than Whites convicted of similar crimes. This is directly evidenced in the 100 to 1 sentencing quantity disparity for crack cocaine versus powder cocaine. That was not always the case. But American standards have a way of changing according to the whims of the most powerful forces within our society.

Like crack cocaine sentencing, the threshold for the death penalty may find itself on a sliding scale. The list of circumstances that make one death penalty eligible may change to include those habitual offenders convicted of their third strike. It may be them on death row today, but it may be you tomorrow.

The people did not give the Criminal Justice system the power to mead out punishment that is cruel nor unusual. The judges, lawyers, and injured parties are not authorized to seek revenge. The only protection people have against tyranny is the precept that we are a nation of laws. As such, even when emotions run high, the overriding responsibility of the Justice system is to safeguard the public, and provide remedies within the confines of the law.

Even in a case where a sick or depraved human being commits a heinous act, whether motivated by passion or greed, society must exercise restraint. We cannot take a life under thoughtful circumstances and call ourselves civilized.

-1-

THE STATE MAKES MISTAKES

Death is final and irreversible. Once the state pulls the switch there is no way back. Right this very moment, there are men and women on Death Row for crimes they may not have committed.

Since 1973, one hundred-twenty seven Death Row inmates have been exonerated and subsequently released from custody. These people were scheduled for execution. Their lives would have been taken if not for the improved forensics and modern technologies that enabled improved analysis of DNA evidence.

The well-documented failure of our criminal justice system to protect the rights of the innocent makes it is impossible to justify the execution of any human being. It is better to let nine guilty people live in prison isolation for life, than to kill one innocent person.

-2-

LIGHT SKIN V. DARK SKIN

Colorism is *"a type of discrimination against certain human beings within the same racial group, based solely upon skin tone."* This is the most superficial form of discrimination since skin tone is determined only by the amount of melanin in the skin. It has nothing to do with intellect or proclivity.

This behavior was first practiced by slave owners. The dark skinned slaves were made to work in the field; Whereas, light skinned slaves were chosen to work in the house. This Colorism phenomenom is not to be confused with the psychological distinction of House Negros and Field Negros, based upon mindset not skin color.

During the early 1900s, many exclusive African American organizations utilized the Brown Paper Bag Test to screen candidates for admission. A brown paper bag was placed next to the skin of applicants. Those with skin darker than the paper bag were denied affiliation. Some Black Greek organizations were notoriously guilty of this practice.

This light skinned dark skinned division continued throughout the sixties, seventies and the eighties. Employers and others in positions of authority demonstrated partiality towards African Americans with light skin and good hair. This factor resulted in increased sales of skin bleaching agents. The extreme change in Michael Jackson's appearance is a famous example of how far some African Americans will go to gain acceptance.

Evidence of Colorism has even been noted in the justice system. The majority of the prisoners on death row are African American. According to the Journal of Blacks in Higher Education, *Issue No. 51 (Spring 2006),*

"54% Percent of all African Americans with dark skin who were convicted of murdering a white person were sentenced to death; whereas, 24% Percent of all African Americans with light skin who were convicted of murdering a white person were sentenced to death."

This was confirmed by the findings of Jennifer Eberhardt, whose research was supported by grants from the Stanford Center for Social Innovation and the National Science Foundation. The results were published in the May issue of the journal Psychological Science entitled *Looking Deathworthy: Perceived Stereotypicality of Black Defendants Predicts Capital-Sentencing Outcomes.*

"Male murderers with stereotypically 'black-looking' features are more than twice as likely to get the death sentence than lighter-skinned African American defendants found guilty of killing a white person, Stanford researchers have found. The relationship between physical appearance and the death sentence disappears, however, when both murderers and their victims are black."

The mantra for leaders in the 1960s, 70s and 80s was, "if you're not on television, you don't exist."

CHAPTER 35

MODERN LEADERSHIP CHALLENGES

*T*his nation constantly grapples with its responsibility to keep its citizens safe. Similarly, leaders maneuver to safeguard their supporters. This is the greatest challenge facing a modern leader. As we saw with the hippie movement of the 60's, as a rule, people are not eager to risk their well being for any cause.

One exception to this rule was the non-violent Civil Rights Movement, led by the charismatic Dr. Martin Luther King, Jr., which dominated the late 1950s, and 60s. Marchers who participated in those demonstrations showed up, braced for the worst. Through fearless perseverance, they ultimately won the battle for civil rights, voting rights, and human dignity.

Another notable exception to the rule was the labor union movement of the late 1800s. The violent nature of that struggle is best exemplified by the May 1886 Haymarket Riot in Chicago, which left several police and protestors dead.

Those dissident workers were motivated by the fact that they felt safer on the picket lines than they did on their jobs. Their resolve ultimately resulted in improved worker's rights, including an eight-hour workday.

-1-

SOUND AN EFFECTIVE ALARM

The second most critical challenge facing modern leaders is sounding an impassioned alarm that gets the attention of the masses. In today's complex society, there is no shortage of competent leaders or worthy causes. The airwaves, highways and byways are cluttered with all kinds of appeals - *passionate pleas for support.*

There is a limited amount of space on the average person's plate for consideration of matters that may not directly impact them or members of their immediate family. Thus, most people have become proficient at quickly categorizing unsolicited appeals and reacting to them accordingly. A critical message may never be heard if the leader fails to hook people with their initial appeal.

The most effective appeals crisply touch the heart and soul of the hearer and create a kinship. Typically, appeals to help find missing persons, or even missing animals, pique human interest and generate a high level of response. In general, appeals that evoke empathy result in recruitment opportunities On the other hand, convoluted appeals of little or no personal relevance usually fall upon deaf ears.

-2-

FOOLPROOF MESSAGE

The third most critical challenge facing modern leaders is to craft and deliver an analytical message that is foolproof. A leader must do more than simply sound the alarm to get people's attention. They must explain the gravity of the situation, demonstrate its universal relevance, identify the goal, outline an action plan that is narrowly drawn to quickly accomplish the mission, and suggest immediate steps even the willing untrained can take. The most effective leaders are able to accomplish all of these objectives in one breath.

To be effective, a leader must remain calm under pressure and keep the focus on the positive, even while urgently sounding an alarm. Flight attendants serve as a good example. (No pun intended.) They are much more than highflying wait staff. Like any other leader, their first job is to ensure the safety of all passengers.

For example, in the event of an emergency the flight attendant, consistent with their training, will use the intercom to calmly explain: "Ladies and gentlemen, you may have noticed there is smoke in the cabin. The captain is aware and has turned on the fasten seatbelt sign. We will be landing shortly. Please fasten your seatbelts, return your tray table to its upright position and stow any items under the seat in front of you. Now is a good time to look around and locate the nearest emergency exit. Once we are on the ground and the aircraft has come to a complete stop please proceed to that exit in a calm and orderly manner. If you are seated in an exit row, please wait until the plane comes to a complete stop before you open the exit door. Once the chute inflates cross your arms over your chest and jump feet first. I look forward to greeting each of you once we are safely away from the aircraft."

If the leader panics at the slightest sign of trouble, the result is sure to be pandemonium. The captain sets the tone. A captain, who is not prepared to go down with the ship, should remain on dry land.

To achieve exposure and maximize impact, a leader must widely disseminate their message. Whenever a message is released into the public domain the danger exists that reporters or repeaters will take it out of context. That danger is greater when the message is verbal as opposed to written.

If the message reflects negatively on the messenger, the ensuing debate may overshadow its intent. Many leaders have found themselves embroiled in a media storm, attempting to clarify their true intention. If a leader is forced to spend time defending their character, the focus is invariably on the messenger and off of the message. Consequently, the cause is hindered.

To insulate a decidedly complex message and protect its integrity, media savvy leaders rely upon redundancy - simultaneous release to multiple media sources. It is difficult, if not impossible for several reporters to misinterpret a message or similarly misrepresent its context. The odds are pretty good that some of them will get it right. Those that get it right counter balance those that get it wrong. Therefore, redundancy may be the best means of refuting an erroneous report and thereby minimizing the negative impact.

Advancing technology is a dual edged sword, which presents a great opportunity and equally as great a challenge to modern leaders. Advanced technology presents the unfettered opportunity to broadcast a message, as well as the unconstrained opportunity for strangers to distort that message. High tech hackers have become proficient at altering technology-based postings of all kinds. Therefore, in addition to carefully couching their message to withstand all scrutiny, today's leaders must shield that message to protect it from high tech assault.

Martin L. "Daddy" King, Sr. often exclaimed, "Make It Plain; Make It Plain." The more important the message; the more pertinent Daddy King's refrain.

CHAPTER 36

CLINTON-GAFFE

*P*rior to the utterance or release of any silver bullet statement – *one designed to take the wind out of an opponent's sails* - that message should be critiqued by a diverse group of able advisors. Both the statement (substance, tone and tenor), and all aspects of the presentation (audience, time and place), should then be vetted and tweaked in response to the feedback of the group. Adherence to this principle will help to make any message foolproof, thus reducing the likelihood that it will be misconstrued.

During the 2008 campaign for the Democratic Nomination, would be first husband, Former President William Jefferson Clinton, failed to adhere to this principle and the campaign of Hillary paid a hefty price. Immediately after Barack Obama's sweeping victory in the South Carolina primary, Bill Clinton propounded the obvious by commenting that Rev. Jesse Jackson had won that state in the 1984 and 1988 Democratic primaries. Clearly, Clinton's intention was to frame the discussion, put it into perspective, and thereby, forestall the media's penchant to make a mundane victory appear monumental.

However, before Clinton's statement could resonate, the Obama forces countered and painted it as race bating. Although Clinton had made his point and minimized the importance of that victory, he lost cool points with a lot of African Americans who once revered him.

Any leader's first goal must be to do no harm. Clinton-Gaffe resulted in the most significant shift in momentum experienced by either campaign. Bill Clinton's perceived slight awakened a sleeping beast and galvanized African Americans in a way that Obama had, heretofore, been unable to. From that point forward, African Americans didn't simply line-up behind Senator Barack Obama, they lined-up against Senator Hillary Clinton. Because of Clinton-Gaffe, the campaign became personal.

A focus group might have reminded Bill Clinton that the media is always looking for sour grapes. Therefore, a leader should be respectful, deferential and conciliatory especially in defeat. That group might have also warned Clinton that his approach was blatantly obvious and that his reaction had most likely been anticipated by the Obama camp, which probably had ready-made talking points that cried foul. Furthermore, it appeared to marginalize South Carolina's large African American voting base.

With that in mind, Clinton should have been content to highlight Hillary's positives, promote the viability of the campaign, and display and air of inevitability. A focus group might have suggested that Bill Clinton give a statement along these lines: "I applaud Barack Obama who did as well as I expected he would winning South Carolina. However, I am extremely pleased with the vote Hillary received. Not only did she do better than expected among her core constituency, she expanded her base of support, and increased her delegate count."

By so doing, Clinton would have given the media the pencil, and allowed them to fill in the blanks. Even without his input, their analysis would have included the obvious comparisons between the Jackson and Obama victories.

Some shined shoes got holes in their soles.

CHAPTER 37

COSBY POUND CAKE DEBACLE

*I*n May 2004, controversy erupted after comedic actor Bill Cosby delivered his infamous "Pound Cake" speech before an audience commemorating the 50th Anniversary of the Brown v. Board of Education landmark decision. At this celebration of the U.S. Supreme Court's rejection of school segregation, Cosby harangued African Americans, whom he claims are not holding up their end of the deal. Cosby's failed foray into leadership on this dignified occasion provides us a great case study.

Many people with no real connection to socially and economically deprived African Americans share the critical views expressed by Bill Cosby. Generally speaking, those critics fail to recognize that all people are not treated equal. When it comes to the impact of Institutional Racism, poorer African Americans are the "canary in the coal mine."

In his speech, Cosby initially identified the object of his ire as "the lower economic and lower middle economic people." However, it quickly became apparent that he was referring specifically to African Americans within those classifications. Throughout his speech, Mr. Cosby found it easier to blame African American people, than to confront the social system that threatens the quality of African American life.

-1-

PARENTAL AUTONOMY

Cosby used colorful colloquialisms to demonstrate the lack of parenting by those in the lower economic stratum of the African American community. Yet, he completely ignored the fact that society has enacted measures that severely restrict a parent's right to discipline their child. Many of the practices that proved successful in the past have been outlawed.

At a very early age, children are instructed that no one, including a parent, has the right to yell at them, or spank them. Each state's department of children services promotes a 1-800 hotline number for children to contact authorities in the event they feel violated or abused. Every such call is taken seriously. Once a case is reported, parents are subject to investigation and detailed scrutiny. Some examiners are "Monday morning quarterbacks," prone to unfairly judge parents.

I am not a proponent of liberal corporal punishment. However, I am in favor of parental autonomy. I am an advocate for an involved society capable of interceding to prevent abuse especially within the family unit. However, I understand how important it is for parents to have the latitude to employ persuasive measures to ensure their child's positive behavior.

Rather than blame a complete class of parents, Cosby should have shed light on the system that has deprived good parents of the ability to impose their will upon children who are in constant need of supervision and guidance.

-2-

UNJUSTIFIED HOMICIDE

In his haste to blame African American people, by his own words, Cosby condemned the system he sought to uphold. The facts speak for themselves. He comically opined,

> "Looking at the incarcerated, these are not political criminals. These are people going around stealing Coca Cola. People getting shot in the back of the head over a piece of pound cake! And then we all run out and are outraged, *'The cops shouldn't have shot him.'* What the hell was he doing with the pound cake in his hand? I wanted a piece of pound cake just as bad as anybody else. And I looked at it and I had no money. And something called parenting said, 'if you get caught with it you're going to embarrass your mother.' Not 'you're going to get your butt

kicked.' No. 'You're going to embarrass your family."

It's interesting that in his own situational narrative, Cosby spoke of victims who stole food and drink, not trinkets and jewels. I do not condone stealing. As a general principle, No one has the right to take anything that does not belong to them. However, under certain circumstances people are justified in taking what they need to survive.

For example the survivors of Hurricane Katrina were forced to break into stores to acquire life saving supplies. That was the right thing to do under those circumstances. The law of self-preservation will excuse a desperate person who acts in an, otherwise, asocial manner.

More importantly, when Cosby describes the police response to this alleged theft of food, he notes that these people were shot in the back of the head. The use of deadly force by a police officer is as much an action of last resort as War itself.

At that moment, Cosby was presented with an opportunity to cite statistics that evidence the disproportionate number of police shooting in poorer African American communities.

Too often African Americans are shot in the back or in some other manner that suggests there was no confrontation or threat that warranted the taking of a life. Instead, Cosby chose to point the finger at the victims of these unjustifiable police shooting.

Cosby chose not to highlight the senseless taking of a life, which is the most egregious action a state official can engage in. Instead, in an Establishment voice he asked, "What the hell was he doing with the pound cake in his hand?" Cosby should have asked, "Why did that policeman shoot a child for stealing a Coke and a piece of pound cake?"

Cosby didn't stop there, he also mocked the members of the community who "run out and are outraged." This sinister admonishment had the potential to dispirit those who, unlike bobbleheads, don't close their window shutters and ignore community situations. Cosby seemed to suggest that rather than rally for justice, those concerned neighbors should wait until the body is removed and the blood is wiped up before coming outside.

-3-

OLD STEREOTYPE, NEW LIFE

Cosby went on to castigate an entire community of people. He said, "We cannot blame white people. White people -- white people don't live over there. They close up the shop early. The

Korean ones still don't know us as well -- they stay open 24 hours." In fact, most African Americans are honest and hardworking people. Contrary to Cosby's generalization, we, as a people, do not steal.

The media is more likely than not to focus on inflammatory rhetoric that demeans African Americans. Statements that fit that mold are a premium. There is always space on the front page for American heroes who breathe new life into old African American stereotypes.

Bill Cosby further demonstrated the danger inherent in engaging in generalized characterizations that cast aspersions on entire groups of people. He widened his net, and without qualification, berated professional athletes, by declaring, "Basketball players, multimillionaires, can't write a paragraph. Football players, multimillionaires, can't read." This gratuitous degradation of professionals who have labored to excel in their craft served no useful purpose. In fact, those statements had the potential to diminish them in the hopeful eyes of children, who might otherwise be inspired.

Similarly, Bill Cosby was wrong in his general characterization of the 900,000 African American men and 200,000 African American women who are languishing in jail. Relatively few of them are in prison for the commission of violent crimes. Most are non-violent drug users who pose no serious threat to society. Whites who are convicted of the same crimes are excused. Thus, there is a case to be made that the needlessly incarcerated are in fact political prisoners.

On average, African Americans are serving longer sentences than Whites convicted of similar crimes. In an attempt to remedy this situation, Senator Joe Biden introduced the Drug Sentencing Reform & Kingpin Trafficking Act of 2007. If passed this would help to diminish the Black-White incarceration ratio. In 2004, Cosby could have beaten Biden to the punch and used that occasion to call for such an initiative.

-4-

LEADERS PROVIDE SOLUTIONS

Having chosen to make a political statement, Cosby could have demonstrated real leadership and boldly challenged the system that warehouses non-violent drug offenders and petty thieves. He could have pointed out the need for more mental health intervention centers, drug treatment and rehabilitation facilities; or the need to provide the incarcerated an education, vocation, or the skill training necessary to prepare them to be productive citizens upon release. Instead Cosby chose to kick them while they were down.

Undoubtedly, Cosby's celebrity status provides him a lofty platform from which to sound an alarm. However, name recognition or the ability to get people's attention, do not automatically make one a leader. When provided the opportunity, one who would be a leader must make statements that make sense.

Cosby suggested we have to take our neighborhoods back, and begin to build businesses in our community. Historically, lending institutions have unfairly denied qualified African Americans the capital needed to build such establishments. The community is in need of an action plan that would facilitate access to capital. Cosby failed to suggest such a plan and did not offer his celebrity status as a means of calling attention to this concern.

A well-known personality that sounds an alarm must do more than prove they have a loud mouth or a big platform. They must offer meaningful solutions. Otherwise, they serve as a Detractor, not as a Leader.

Soon, we will reminisce about this fiction called freedom the same way elders of every generation reminisce about the "good old days."

CONCLUSION

I recently went to the Illinois State Thompson Center. I got on the elevator in the lobby and got off on my designated floor. I was asked by the State security guard to show my State I.D. I did not hesitate to comply. Still I thought how these newfangled security measures pose a hardship on persons who have no State issued I.D., but have business to conduct within the State building.

Yesterday, I returned to the State of Illinois building. Things had changed drastically since my aforementioned visit. They had implemented new beefed up security procedures. Anyone seeking to get on the elevators was required to empty their pockets and dump all items into a large plastic bin for inspection; and then walk through a metal detector. That did not sit well with me. Those security procedures obviously were not about security at all. Like the airport liquid restrictions, it was a weak attempt at providing a false sense of security.

The cavernous lobby of the Thompson center is wide open all the way up to the 16th floor, and also wide open to the magnificent concourse level easily visible below. The concourse level has a food court with seating for approximately 1,000 people. There were 2,000 people in the spacious lobby and the packed concourse level. There was no screening required to access those areas with huge numbers of people. A terrorist or others seeking to do damage to the building or harm to the people therein, would have ample opportunity to do so. If it were truly about security, the building lobbies with large concentrations of people would be the focus of protection efforts.

Because of the new TSA security procedures, passengers must arrive 2 to 3 hours before their scheduled flight time. That means more people, including the hordes of TSA agents, now spend more time in the terminals. Thus there are unprecedented numbers of people in airport terminals at any given time. Certainly more than all of the people on all of the flights combined. If the actual goal were to prevent a terrorist attack or minimize its potential, we would not create circumstances that put more people at risk.

Many court buildings have stringent security requirements. The stated goal is to protect the judges, lawyers, staff and litigants. However, we have no plan to protect those valued members of our society once they are outside of the building. We must find more sensible ways to protect the citizens of this great nation from foreign and domestic threats, without circumventing the rights of law-abiding citizens.